226

226

How I Became the First Blind Person to Kayak the Grand Canyon

Lonnie Bedwell
with Joel Canfeld

Pro Player Publishing

WILMINGTON, DELAWARE

Pro Player Publishing
300 Delaware Avenue
Wilmington, DE 19801
www.ProPlayerPress.com

Ordering Information:
Quantity sales. Special discounts are available on quantity purchases by corporations, associations, and others. For details, contact the "Special Sales Department" at the address above.

226 / Lonnie Bedwell with Joel Canfeld. -- 1st ed.
ISBN 978-0981471099

CONTENTS

How this Book Came to Be

by Richard Seppala

It was late 2013. I was at a marketing conference, where I had a booth set up to interest prospective customers. This wasn't the first time I had done this – as a matter of fact, it was very much business as usual for me. But what was about to happen was…well, very unusual.

It was early in the morning and I was pretty much by my lonesome – not many people in the hall yet. But then I saw this guy walking around. He was wearing sunglasses indoors at 7 am. I thought to myself, "Okay, cool, he thinks he's Jack Nicholson at a Lakers game. Either that, or he's hung over."

Anyway, Mr. Shades made his way over to my booth and started chatting me up. He wanted to know what I did. I told him that I billed myself as "The ROI Guy," and I helped small businesses optimize their marketing by using customized technology designed to help them track their customers, sales and ad placements. It was all about helping increase my clients' ROI (Return on Investment).

He said that sounded interesting – and then he asked, "Can you help me?" I shrugged. "Well, tell me what you're trying to do and I'll see if I can." He answered, "I'm trying to get my story out."

Well, that wasn't what the kind of thing I usually did, but he intrigued me – so I asked what exactly his story *was*. That's when he told me he was the first blind person to ever kayak over the whitewater rapids of the Colorado River through the entire Grand Canyon.

Whoa.

Two powerful things suddenly hit me at once.

First of all, this dude was blind and I never even noticed because of the way he had been walking around so easily and confidently, without a service dog or companion to help guide him.

Second of all, my father-in-law, after he learned he had ALS (also known as Lou Gehrig's disease), had done the exact same trip despite his deteriorating physical condition. He too had triumphed over his disability in the same way.

I asked him, "So you're totally blind?"

"Yep," he said, "Totally blind."

He told me his name was Lonnie Bedwell, and, as he talked about his historic Grand Canyon trip, I wondered what motivated him to take on such an extreme challenge. He told me he did it for two reasons. First of all, he wanted to raise public awareness of the plight of disabled veterans – of which there were plenty after America's lengthy conflicts in Iraq and Afghanistan. The volunteer vets organization Team River Runner had sponsored the trip and he wanted to help raise money for it. Secondly, he wanted to show these disabled veterans what was possible if they took advantage of these kinds of nonprofit programs. Many of them still suffered from depression because of their severe injuries and he wanted to help them make a new start.

Because of my lifelong love of being on the water, combined with the emotional connection to my father-in-law's Grand Canyon trip, I felt obliged to help Lonnie share his story with the world - especially after I heard the whole thing, because what Lonnie told me turned out to be one of the most amazing personal accounts I had ever heard in my life.

With my knowledge and experience, I've helped many businesses build awareness through successful branding efforts; I decided that skill-set would come in handy when it came to Lonnie. I also figured out that the best way to really share Lonnie's adventures was to *show* them. I had already produced a few documentaries and I told Lonnie that if he ever did anything crazy like kayaking through the Grand Canyon again, he should give me a call and I would set up a film crew to film the whole thing.

Well, three months later, Lonnie called and said, "Richard, if you're serious, we're doing another whitewater kayaking trip in Montana through Yellowstone National Park." I was serious and we filmed the whole thing, which is now a feature-length documentary titled, *On Me*.

After the filming was done, I knew we needed to have another component in place to fully tell Lonnie's tale. I said to him, "Lonnie, you need a book. You need a place to really tell your complete story so people understand who you are and what you've had to go through to get to where you are today."

The result is what you're reading right this minute. And trust me, it's a great read.

Lonnie has been helping inspire a lot of his fellow veterans with his exploits and, whenever someone asks him if it makes him feel good to help them, his reply is always the same: Those veterans did him and all of us a favor by fighting for us and he's just paying them back.

That's how I feel about Lonnie – I may have set up this book and the documentary, but I have gotten a lot more out of knowing him than he has from knowing me. The biggest thing is, when I'm having a hard day and something's not going right, I will literally stop and think about what Lonnie did – kayak through some of the toughest whitewater rapids blind, never quitting and never complaining. Thinking about his accomplishments really motivates me to suck it up, stop complaining, and just focus and drive through whatever small problem I might be having. And that comes in handy on a daily basis.

This book and the documentary are my way of paying Lonnie back for his courage, his example and his inspiration. And frankly, Lonnie should be an inspiration to everybody. When he goes on his whitewater adventures, his viewpoint is this: Failure is not an option, and if you do get knocked down, you just get back up into the boat and keep paddling. Just because you get flipped over in the river doesn't mean the trip is over. You just have to learn how to roll back up and keep moving on.

The spirit of that lesson resonated with me as a businessperson, husband, and father – and I hope it resonates with you as you read Lonnie's incredible story in the following pages.

Richard Seppala
April, 2015

Foreword

by Alex Nielson

I still remember my first awkward moments in a whitewater kayak. I was 23-years-old and had just returned home after five years of duty as a combat medic with two tough tours in Iraq and Afghanistan. I was young, fragile, and desperately in need of some form of escape. In that vulnerable place the river spoke to me. Looking back, I know the river saved me.

We are all drawn to the river for different reasons, but I believe it is the people we meet on the water that keep us coming back time and time again. Lonnie is one of those people. No matter the situation, he always has a joke and a smile. As apprehensive as I felt guiding him down the Colorado River during his historic journey in 2013, I never once saw him lose his nerve. Always calm, always patient, Lonnie remains a shining example of inner strength and humility.

Without cell phones or electricity to distract us at night, we talked about our lives and about the things that had brought us together. We talked about the river and about our strategy for the trip, but mostly we just talked. Lonnie told me about his life in the Navy and in school, and how he had raised his family. I told him about my life and the things that scared me the most about the future.

In those moments it was as if the world outside of our little expedition simply vanished in the ether. It did not matter that Lonnie was blind and that he was trusting me with his life at times, in the Grand Canyon we were simply two good paddling buddies sharing an experience. I believe that it was this mutual respect and our close friendship that played the most important role in our success on the water.

In the end, as much as Lonnie and I both wanted to successfully complete the entire Grand Canyon, our trip was really about something larger and more beautiful than a singular accomplishment. Over the last few years, murmurs of Lonnie's adventure have spread like wildfire, and it seems like wherever I go someone is talking about a blind guy that kayaked the Grand Canyon. Inspired by Lonnie, more blind kayakers are taking to their local rivers and ponds. Each time these new paddlers master a new technique, or meet a new friend through the sport, the success of our trip grows a little more.

Despite this success, there are also many critics. The river is a beautiful thing, but it is also dangerous. I have lost friends to the water and have been a part of more than one close call. Experienced paddlers who I respect have questioned the safety of taking blind kayakers down large-volume rapids. In a sport where a single misplaced paddle stroke can lead to a life-or-death situation, I wholeheartedly agree with them in many ways. But there was an intangible magic about our time in the canyon that cannot be easily accounted for by those who were not there. If only they knew the whole story; how the trip actually went down, how decisions were made, how we depended on each other, and how we trusted each other with our lives – only then would they understand just how crazy the whole thing actually was.

In this book, Lonnie tells that story, with the help of me and some others on the trip. He also tells his own personal and inspiring story of how he not only overcame the trauma of his blindness, but also helped other veterans similarly afflicted learn to overcome theirs.

You can learn a lot from Lonnie. I did. I learned so much from him that by the end of our time together in the Grand Canyon, I realized that the trip was really as much about Lonnie guiding me as it was about me guiding Lonnie.

Alex Nielson
April, 2015

Lonnie and Alex

Introduction

Lonnie Kayaking on Colorado River Rapids
(Photo by Marc Huster)

226.

That's the number of miles it takes to get through the Grand Canyon on the Colorado River. Many of those miles will take you through whitewater rapids that are incredibly strong, some of the strongest in the world. If you want to kayak through those rapids, the experts say you should first have years and years of training. There's a reason for that - more than a few boaters have died in the attempt to travel those 226 miles.

I had only been kayaking for around a year when I took my turn on the Colorado. Worse, I only had fourteen days of practice on actual whitewater rapids.

Third strike? I'm "lights-out" blind.

In spite of all that, I had the honor of being the first sightless person ever to kayak down the totality of those 226 miles of dangerous, powerful water. Many people thought it couldn't be done. Fortunately, I was not one of them and neither was Joe Mornini, Executive Director and Co-Founder of Team River Runner, the wonderful organization that sponsored me in this effort (which you'll be hearing a great deal about in this book).

Of course, you never know for sure you can do something until you actually give it a try. It wasn't until around day three of the trip, when I successfully navigated the first major rapids, that my lead guide, Alex Nielson, and I knew for sure someone like me could make it the entire 226 miles. Although my spirits were soaring at that point, I had yet to be tested by the worst of the rapids, including the infamous Lava Falls, the rapids that even the most experienced kayakers approach with butterflies in their stomachs. I didn't know that my lack of sleep, combined with a defective kayak, would almost stop me for good on Day 8. Nor, on Day 15, did I anticipate my boat getting shot out of the water like a cannonball – causing its sightless occupant to do a complete backflip in the middle of the air and end up with his sunglasses getting cracked in half by a mile marker.

Yeah, I'm talking about me.

The truth is, in the 16 days it took to make the trip, I experienced every kind of extreme emotion a human being can feel. Joy, triumph, anger, defeat, exhaustion, and more than a little bit of nerves here and there. It's hard to fully describe everything I went through during this trip, but I'll do my best – and fortunately, I'll have the help of three great guys who went along for the ride: U.S. Navy veteran Alex Nielson and Army vets Leonard "Chip" Sell and Michael Bradley. These three men all bravely served their country overseas in the Iraq and Afghanistan conflicts - and I was lucky enough to have them guiding me down the river, making sure I stayed afloat most of the time (although, as you'll see, I did get my head wet more than once!). Their assistance was invaluable to my efforts, and I have asked them to provide their perspectives on the events of the kayaking trip as well.

In fact, I want to make it clear that my historic feat was far from my accomplishment alone – I simply could not have succeeded in this crazy quest if it weren't for the amazing fifteen men and women who also made the trip with me. All of them went out of their way to help me in every way possible, both on and off the river, and I thank God that such a wonderful group was there with me to provide a level of teamwork I'd never experienced since I myself left the military.

I'm also going to talk about my life leading up to the Grand Canyon trip, so you can understand a little bit more about me and what led me to take on this kind of challenge. To help with that effort, you'll be hearing from a few other people who have been important to me over the years, people who are near and dear to me and have always been there when I needed them. I am happy they are participating in this project, because they can give you their own perspectives on the events of my life.

There are two reasons I chose to write this book. The first reason? So others with physical disabilities such as mine can understand what is possible. When you're in this situation, you have two choices in life: Live in fear and pity - or just *live*. I'm always incredibly grateful when someone tells me that I inspired them to keep moving, keep growing and enjoy life again. I hope this book helps someone else like me achieve his or her dreams.

The second reason I wrote this book is just as important: to call attention to the plight of the men and women of our country's armed services who have served above and beyond the call of duty in two difficult wars. One of five veterans who served in Iraq and/or Afghanistan was wounded during his or her tour of duty and deserves whatever support we can give him or her in his or her effort to resume civilian life. Programs like the Team River Runner organization provide crucial help to those veterans' minds, bodies and spirits by providing positive physical activities geared to their specific needs. You'll hear from some veterans in this book about how Team River Runner made an incredible difference to their mental attitudes, and, in some cases, turned them in a positive direction for the first time since returning home from the front.

Finally, I'd like to thank you for taking time to read my story. Growing up as a country boy in Indiana, I hardly expected to end up writing a book like this. I hope you enjoy reading about my journey as much as I've enjoyed living it.

Chapter One

Growing Up Country

The first time I beat death, I was way too young to appreciate the victory.

That's because I was just a baby, about 22 months old. While my mother was cooking something on the stove, she happened to go outside for a few moments. While she was gone, a giant grease fire erupted. The whole kitchen was soon in flames, and my mother couldn't get back inside.

Meanwhile, my brother Larry and I were up in our rooms. Now, Larry wasn't much more help than I was – he was not quite 3 years old. Nobody could get to us, because the fire had spread so quickly. Finally, one of our neighbors came over and, according to my mom, climbed on his wife's back to get into our window. He got me out of the crib and handed me down. I had to be resuscitated, but, thankfully, I came back to life without a problem. My brother was harder to track down – he was already mobile and could walk (and, when he was really ambitious, even run). But our neighbor finally found him. Since he was in the burning house a lot longer than I, he was in worse shape than me. We both needed to be in an oxygen tent for a couple of days. Luckily, we both recovered fully.

The house where that happened is still standing just a quarter mile from where I currently live. But we never lived in it again after that incident. My mother would NOT move back in there – and we ended up moving to nearby Pleasantville, 6 or 7 miles away. Population? About 120 people.

Me with a friend I found in the backyard

Obviously, I'm not from the big city. Or any kind of city. My roots are in rural Indiana. If you look for Pleasantville on Google Maps, you'll see a whole lot of green around our little town, because we have a lot of protected wildlife area – and a lot of blue, because there are a ton of rivers, ponds, creeks and lakes. Hunting and fishing is a way of life where I'm from – I can't remember ever not doing it. It's what I grew up with, along with a lot of country music and, most importantly, a lot of great family and friends.

I was born June 19, 1965, in Sullivan Hospital in nearby Sullivan, Indiana, the second of two boys. My parents are Jerry Bedwell and Sherry Smith-Bedwell, and to understand me, you have to understand them.

Ma was a housewife her entire life. When I think of her, I think of her smiling – because she's always got a grin on her face, just like my dad. She loves to joke and laugh and I certainly share those traits. She has also been completely content with being a housewife – because she never runs out of things to do. That's because when you're obsessive-compulsive about cleaning, you're never done taking care of the house! Yes, she always loved to clean, but hated to cook (even though she was good at it). When I was growing up, you could literally eat off any of the floors in the house; they were that spotless. And so were we, when she finally got her hands on us. When she wanted to take a nice picture of my brother and me when we were little, it was a five step process that went like this:

Step 1: Go outside and spread a towel out over the ground.

Step 2: Get us dressed up in our nice clothes and our little patent white shoes.

Step 3: Carry us out of the house and put us down on that towel in the yard.

Step 4: Take the picture.

Step 5: Carry us back *into* the house and throw the towel in the washer.

Lonnie and Larry - Step 4

Of course, with raising two boys, dirt was definitely going to make its way to her doorstep. She's still got the pictures of when my cousin and I went riding our bikes after a rainstorm and decided to pedal as fast as we could through as many mud puddles as we could find. We came back covered head-to-toe with the stuff to the point where we were unrecognizable as human beings. And that was only the start of how we drove her nuts. Larry and I would often come back filthy from our hunting and fishing escapades and she was the one who had to deal with the dirt – not to mention my countless injuries!

Lonnie's Mom: *Lonnie, when he was little, every injury that kid ever had, it seemed like it was to his head. When he was little, he was running around the yard while wearing his father's coal-miner hard hat. He tripped and fell and knocked his two front teeth out on the hat.*

Another time, he was playing in the backyard at his cousin's house. There were blankets over the clothesline and Lonnie ran full-speed through one of those blankets and right into the clothesline pole on the other side. He hit it right between his eyes, and ended up with two big black eyes - he looked like he had been in a car wreck.

Then there was the time Lonnie went and got stung by over a hundred bees. He was playing with his brother down by a ditch and they slid down the dirt into it. Suddenly, he come running to the house, covered solid with bees, except for his glasses. We ran water over him in the tub, then got him to the hospital and he probably had over one hundred stings. If he had been allergic to bee stings, it would have killed him. The only place that kid didn't have a sting was where he had his glasses on!

One of my many childhood injuries.

Somehow I survived all that. Luckily, as I said, Ma always could laugh at our youthful misadventures – and herself. Most importantly, she still has a heart of gold, and that heart revolves around her family; it really does.

When I was in the Navy and deployed on a submarine, it was Christmastime. And when you're underwater for Christmas, it can really dampen your holiday spirit (especially if you stick your head out the window...). So she sent me a miniature Christmas tree, about 2 feet tall, to cheer us all up. Well, I put it up in the sub and all the guys on the crew started decorating it with whatever they happened to have laying around. It turned out to be a very special symbol to all of us, because it reflected all our personalities, and it meant a lot to me personally that I was able to give the crew that little spiritual boost. ,

Yes, Ma is a sweet lady who made sure to take us to church every Sunday when we were younger. She didn't stand for getting into scrapes either. She always told us to avoid fights, probably because my dad was so good at getting into them. She would say, "Don't fight. Every time you can, walk away. Walk away."

But even she had her limits. One kid was always picking on my brother Larry, day after day, and wouldn't let up on him. And finally Ma said, "All right, enough's enough! You go down there and you thump his butt!" And my brother and I, well, our jaws dropped to the ground and we were like, "Whoa, Mom! Where is *this* coming from?" This is another thing she laughs about to this day, following the chuckle with, "I never should have done that. I never should have done that."

When I think of my mother, I always hear the chorus from the Randy Travis song, "Angels":

Are you telling me that you've never seen an angel?
Never felt the presence of one standing by?

No robe of white
No halo in site
Well you missed the most obvious thing
Man, are you blind?
Just look in your mother's eyes.

Now, my dad? He's not really what most people would call "sweet."

Dad was kind of a jack-of-all-trades. He was a meat cutter for about seven years, and then he began doing union construction for the local coal mines, building tipples and drag lines. After two years of doing that as a day laborer, he got a permanent job with one of the mines doing all sorts of stuff – he was a mechanic welder, he drove a bulldozer, he was a pumper and he did whatever else was required of him.

Dad's a very, very good man. He worked hard and provided well for us. But...well, he's kind of a character. A *rowdy* character. A jokester. The people around home all think he's a comedian. Growing up, all my friends thought he was hilarious – he'd start talking in a Daffy Duck voice or doing some other kind of weird stuff, and they'd laugh their heads off.

But there was a flip side to that fun.

Dad could also be very stern and strict. I remember when I went into the military and they warned me about crossing the company commander, because he could be a real hard ass. My reaction? "Eh, no big deal. You ain't met my dad." I don't think my father had to discipline me but a few times because it stuck real fast. When your father says to you, "If you do that again, I'm gonna tan your hides," you make it a point to work at not doing that again.

And if you think my dad was just a paper tiger, tough with us kids but a shrinking violet out in the world, you need to hear this story. When I was around 11 or 12, some motorcycle gangs came to town. They took over a local highway and forced anybody trying to drive through on it to pay a toll. Obviously, they were just intimidating motorists into handing some money over to them, but their menacing glares and big choppers were doing the trick.

Well, along came Larry, me and my dad in our truck, ready to go ahead and drive down that particular highway. Suddenly, we heard motorcycles driving up and surrounding us – before we knew it, they were in front of us and to the side of us and were intent on stopping us, so they could shake us down. After all, it worked with everybody else on the road, what was so different about us?

What was different was my dad. He looked over at my brother and me and said, "Now, how dang dumb do you have to be to think you're going to pull over a pickup truck with a motorcycle?" With that, he just punched the gas and cut the wheel – and motorcycles flew off the road every which way in his wake. I was terrified. I had the feeling he also was a little worried about the consequences of what he had done – because, when we got home, he took out every gun we had in the house, loaded them up and said, "Boys, y'all know how to use them if we have to."

Well, thank goodness we didn't have to, but the point is my father wasn't the kind to run from trouble. Actually, a lot of the time he would run *into* trouble. I remember being in town one time, standing outside a pizza place. On the other side of the railroad tracks from me was a local pub. I heard a guy yelling, "Fight! Fight! Fight!" and pointing over at the pub. Well, a bunch of us ran up to the railroad tracks to see what was going on and once we did, I wasn't so excited anymore. I just thought to myself, "Aw, crap, it's just my dad again."

Yes, the sight of my father using his fists was a very familiar one and so was dealing with his contrary attitude. His nickname around town was "Birdie," because he was quick to give the finger to anyone passing by, but always in a gesture of friendship. To him, it was like a wave, always done in a positive way with a smile on his face. I would say he's mellowed some now that he's in his sixties, but, two or three years ago, our friend got into it with four guys. They got him down on the floor and Dad dived in to go to his defense. And to add to the stupidity, I joined in the fight too. My dad said to me, "What are you doing here?" and I said, "You're in it, aren't you dad? If you're in it, I'm in it."

Yep, a blind guy and a 65-year-old in a brawl. Mom wasn't too pleased with either of us on that day.

I've got two songs that come to mind when I think of my dad. One is Aaron Tippin's "You've Got to Stand for Something or You'll Fall for Anything" – which contains the line, "You've got to be your own man, not a puppet on a string." That is just absolutely my father's philosophy. And the other song that makes me think of him is Holly Dunn's "Daddy's Hands," especially when she sings, "His hands are not always gentle, but I've come to understand there's always love in my daddy's hands." That's also my dad to a T. Nobody who knows him would ever guess it, but there was many a time when I would find him in deep thought reading the Bible. He's got a heart that's as huge as all of Texas and he would give his life for his family. My mother would too. I was fortunate to have two very compassionate, very kind, very giving people for my parents.

I was also fortunate to have Larry for my older brother, although maybe I didn't feel that way when we were growing up! I had a lot of respect for him, but, like a lot of brothers, we were at each other's throats a lot when we were young. Being younger, I took the most crap – literally. One time he had gone number 2 in his diaper, and, apparently he was in an artistic mood, because he used my face as a canvas and smeared his diaper contents all over my face. And I mean, *smeared*. When he was done, all you could see of me was my blue eyes and my smile. Yes, my smile, because I was too young to think it was all anything but fun. Larry laughs about it to this day and says, "No wonder dad always called you 'shithead.'"

> Lonnie's Mom: *Lonnie loved to aggravate his brother. Larry would set up his toys to play, and Lonnie would stand there real quiet. As soon as Larry was done getting everything where he wanted, Lonnie would run through them and knock 'em all down.*

We fought and argued so much growing up, our mom finally had to take action. This is going to sound like something you might have seen on a sitcom, but it really happened: She went into the bedroom Larry and I shared and used duct tape to split the room right down the middle. The side with Larry's bed was his, the side with my bed was mine, and we were not allowed to cross the line into each other's territory unless we were leaving or entering the room.

It was so crazy that, because the stereo set was in the middle of the room, we each only had access to half of it. I had the volume knob on my side; he had the tuning knob on his side. Now, we liked very different music – I liked country and he was more rock n' roll. So, if I came in and he had his rock music up loud, I turned it way down. If he came in and I had my country station on, he'd turn it to the rock station. On either side, it was not a winnable war.

But when push came to shove, Larry always had my back. If anybody was to pick on me at school, he was there in a heartbeat. I was never what you'd call an imposing presence – I was always a little bitty guy. When I got my first driver's license, I was only 4'11" and weighed 110 pounds. When I graduated high school, I had worked my way all the way up to 5'4" and 120 pounds (and right now, I'm a mammoth 5'8" and 165 pounds). Anyway, when you're a little guy like me, a lot of guys go after you because it's easy pickin's. But if Larry was in earshot, he'd stop the bullies in their tracks.

Today, we're still very close – of course, we sort of have to be, he lives across the road from me now. When he moved in there, my mom asked, "Does that mean I have to put tape down the middle of the road?"

No, Ma, I'm hoping we're past that...

So there's one member of the family I have yet to write about in detail - and that's myself. I guess you could say I was a little feisty, just like my dad and brother. When I was 6 or 7, I remember climbing up a big old maple tree in our front yard. Now this particular maple tree had branches that had grown up in such a perfect arrangement that they actually formed a little wooden bowl in the middle of the top of the tree. I wanted to get into that bowl, so I ran, jumped up off the side of the tree to get some momentum, grabbed a branch, and pulled myself up into it. My mom went looking for me, because she couldn't see where I was from the ground. She walked out and looked in the barn; she walked up the road and just hollered for me over and over. And the whole time I was just sitting up there, watching her.

After about 20 minutes, she was just frantic, not knowing where I was, and yelled with increased urgency. I started feeling bad for her and I finally answered her calls. That's when panic turned to anger. She came over to the tree and screamed, "You get down out of there right now!" My answer? "I'm not coming down until you cool down!"

Then there was the time when I was in Kindergarten and I said in front of the whole class (all of 11 kids!), "Aw, shoot, my mom doesn't do the dishes, she just lets the dogs lick them clean." Well, in a small town, that kind of thing travels fast and Ma hated me for that one. My poor mother. Between my brother, my dad and me, I don't know how she had any sanity left at all.

Cousin Craig with me after our mud puddle marathon

Yes, poor mom - but lucky me, because growing up in that house was wonderful. We only had two acres but we had a barn and a fenced-in yard. In that yard, we usually had a couple of cows, chickens, rabbits and what have you. I remember we had a milk cow named Bessie we used to ride around on and a little pony called Rusty who used to pull a cart. It was fun. We even sort of "adopted" a couple of raccoons. We called one of them Rascal and we took pictures of him on our shoulders.

Another really important part of my upbringing was family – and not just my immediate one. On my dad's side, I'm one of fifteen cousins, and on my mom's side, I'm one of six, along with two second cousins. They weren't like cousins though; they were like brothers and sisters, and almost all of them were in the area. That's what really helped me so much during my darkest days: I have always had such a support system around where I live.

All the Bedwell first cousins – including me – in 2015.

As you can already see, I always had a mischievous streak and that streak didn't end at the school door. I got a few whippings along the way in my hometown education, mostly for the usual kid stuff, like throwing spitballs, but they never caught me for the worst thing I ever did. That involved Skunk Scent, something we hunters would use to mask our smell when we hunted whitetail deer. The kind we had was in two parts, each in its own bottle. On their own, there was nothing noticeable about the liquids, but if you mixed them together...well, the odor was enough to knock you over.

Well, it was the beginning of our senior year in high school, late August or early September, and we were still having really hot summer weather. As our school did not have air conditioning, sitting in one of those classrooms was enough to turn you into a sweaty miserable mess. So, without anybody knowing it, even my friends, I took the two full bottles of the Skunk Scent and I poured them both down under the lockers that went down to the basement, then I walked away.

Well, that got everybody in the school out into the Great Outdoors mighty quick. The smell was really horrible, so they kicked us all out and we ended up having classes on the front lawn and the nearby football field. We did that for two full days while they tried to find the cause – and they never did.

It was a different time back then. My brother and a friend lit an entire brick of firecrackers in the school hallway – like me, they never got caught. Today, if that happened, they'd probably have the whole school on lockdown. I also remember that we'd all pull up to the high school in our cars and trucks with loaded shotguns and .22s hanging in the back. Then, after class was out, we'd go out to hunt. If you showed up with an arsenal like that today, I doubt anybody would be very casual about it.

Still, it wasn't all hijinks and hunting. My dad wouldn't have stood for that. He always made us work, so I always made my own money. Some of that I could earn from hunting and trapping – I could sell the furs of foxes, coyotes and muskrat that I bagged. While I was too young for a regular job, I'd mow yards, shovel horse stalls and put up hay during the summers and do pretty well by it. I'd also split wood and cut firewood for people. In high school and college, I worked for a guy putting in heating and air conditioning units, and learned how to do some electrical wiring.

My dad also stressed that our grades were important, that they "can't take your mind." I took all that to heart and ended up as the Salutatorian of my graduating high school class. The fact is I had to put my competitive drive into academics, because it worked out that I couldn't put it into school sports. My dad got into it with the coach who controlled all three high school sports and the coach took it out on me and my brother. So, in whatever sport I tried, the coach made sure I was made to feel completely miserable about it. It was an unwinnable war, so I quit trying to play sports when I was a freshman.

All that physical energy instead came out when I was behind the wheel. I didn't drink or do drugs – I still have never sampled any illegal substances. Instead, my only vice was that I drove like a maniac. A couple of my cousins always tell the story of being in the car one night when I was flying down a gravel road at 55-60 mph – and because I knew the road so well, I turned off the lights, hit the brakes and started cutting donuts in a big, wide intersection. I guess driving blind like that was just a preview of many years later, when I'd be kayaking through whitewater without a working pair of eyes. Anyway, after I did my donuts, I turned the lights back on and kept going. Unfortunately, the cousin who was riding in the middle with me didn't appreciate my daring and started yelling, "Pull over now!" I was like, "What's the deal?" and he said, "Now! Pull over now!" So I slammed on the brakes and the cousin who was riding shotgun opened the door just in time for him to lean across his lap and throw up on the ground.

The only time I thought I had real trouble one my hands was when I was coming home one night down the 8-mile stretch from Pleasantville to Dugger. I was doing about 90 miles an hour when suddenly, a police car showed up behind me, lights beaming and sirens blaring. So I started slowing down, sure that I was about to get busted big-time.

To my surprise, the cruiser pulled even with me while I was still driving and I saw that my neighbor, who was a county sheriff, was at the wheel. He just flipped me off and kept driving past me! So I slammed the pedal down and drove around him at around 120 mph. Then he came up around me and flew past me again! This kept going on until he led me home to my driveway and came up to me, pointed at me and said, "Now Lonnie, that's your one and only shot. You'd better not do it again."

That was one of the perks of small town living. Your neighbor the cop just might decide to race you rather than arrest you.

So, yeah, it was in many respects pretty much a perfect childhood. But, as many people find, after you graduate from high school, life suddenly gets a lot more complicated - and I was certainly no exception. I was about to face a series of personal challenges that would definitely test me in every possible way.

My brother, Mom, Dad and me. (2015)

Chapter Two

Family and Service

After high school, I followed in my brother Larry's footsteps and went to college at Vincennes University, about a forty-mile drive from where we lived. He went for electronics and lasers, and I went for electronics and robotics, because those were areas that sounded interesting to me.

After graduating from that two-year program, I had to confront a couple of very tough facts. Fact #1 was that there were just no jobs available for me in the area. Fact #2 made Fact #1 a whole lot more of a problem: I now had a wife with a baby on the way whom I needed to support.

I went out with my first wife while attending college and, as happens with many young couples, she ended up pregnant. I was determined to do the right thing and marry her. Obviously, it was not the best way to begin a marriage, but I had no time to reflect on that. I was too concerned about how I was going to take care of my new family – which is why I ended up signing up with the U.S. Navy in 1985, specifically in its nuclear submarine program.

My hitch started with going to the Naval Station Great Lakes, the Navy's only boot camp, located north of Chicago. There, I went to Machinist Mate School, which was supposed to take sixteen weeks. However, since I was allowed to progress at my own speed, I somehow managed to finish it up in just around a week. As a matter of fact, because I finished it so fast, the powers-that-be didn't have anything else for me to do, so I just stayed up there on assignment.

That made it easy for me to come home when my first child was due to be born, a beautiful baby girl we named Courtney. That was a wonderful day. I remember my former mother-in-law was there with a video camera, shooting the whole birth – but when the doctor decided she had to do an episiotomy on my wife, things got a little bloody and, before I knew what was happening, I heard a loud THUMP behind me. My mother-in-law had fainted. As a matter of fact, when you take a look at the video today, all you see of the actual birth is the ceiling!

The nurse who was supposed to be assisting with the birth had to abandon that particular station, because somebody had to make sure my fallen mother-in-law was okay. Meanwhile, the doctor, who was pretty up in years (she delivered me and probably half of Sullivan County), had her hands full and now had nobody to help her out. At the same time, my wife was having a little trouble pushing out the baby. I decided I needed to jump in, so I asked her if I could help coach her through this. My wife looked at me like I was nuts. I needed to reassure her – so I said, "Don't worry, it's okay, I've got plenty of experience helping our cows and pigs give birth."

I learned quickly that it was not wise to compare your wife to a farm animal while she's in labor. It earned me a hard and immediate slap.

However, I still went ahead and did my part, even helping to pull out the placenta after my daughter finally made her way out into the world. I was fortunate to be there for the births of all three of my children, a privilege I wouldn't have traded for any other one in the world.

After my schooling at Great Lakes, I was sent to the nuclear training facility in Orlando, Florida, and then ended far back up north in the Idaho Falls, Idaho, area, where an F-1W submarine prototype had its resting house. I went through the A school there and was told I qualified faster than anybody in the history of that prototype.

I was happy that part of my life was going so well, because the other part wasn't.

A while after my wife gave birth to Ashley, our second daughter, I walked into my home and found myself facing one of the biggest shocks of my life.

My wife was gone. Our kids were gone. Our car was gone.

Also gone? All the money in our bank account – on the day after my payday. I had no money and I wouldn't for a while.

I called my wife at her friend's house, hoping she would be there to explain what had happened. She was. I said, "What's going on?" She told me, "I left, I took the kids and I'm going back to Indiana."

At that moment, I could have compared myself to a farm animal – it was obvious I was the goat here. I had no warning that she was planning to do any of this – and obviously, since she took off while I was on duty, she didn't want me to know her intentions. Now, I was helpless to stop her or at least try to talk about whatever she was feeling inside. She made sure I wouldn't have a chance to do any of that. I didn't have a vehicle and I didn't have a cent to my name – how could I follow her?

More importantly, how was I going to eat? All I had in the house to eat was a bag of potatoes, a loaf of bread, and a jar of peanut butter, none of which were the makings of a gourmet diet.

Nevertheless, that's what I had to make do with. I had to ration out the potatoes, bread and PB until the next payday, so I wouldn't starve. Sure, I could have asked for help, but I was way too embarrassed to tell anybody in my outfit what had happened. Finally, they found out on their own. A navy buddy of mine pulled up one day and saw I was the only one at my house. He asked, "Where'd everybody go?" I told him what had transpired – and about my potato, peanut butter, and bread regimen. I could have pretended it was a trendy diet, but I don't think anybody would have believed me.

My buddy wasn't going to let me live like that, so he got a bunch of the guys together to buy me some groceries. Another guy lent me a truck so I could get around. In the short-term, I could get by until I made it past a few more paydays and was able to start getting back on my feet financially.

That's a common theme in my life – when I get in any kind of trouble, the right people are around to give me a hand. I have been blessed throughout my life with helping hands through a variety of trials and I always have a huge attitude of gratitude about that blessing.

Meanwhile, my domestic drama was far from over. My soon-to-be ex-wife was running wild – and soon, it was pretty obvious I would have to take over custody of our two girls. Since I was stationed far away, my parents temporarily took over their upbringing so they didn't have to be uprooted yet again. I was thankful my folks were willing and able. Soon enough, I was able to come home and visit them on a Temporary Duty Assignment back home, to help with local recruiting efforts.

That assignment directly led me to my next marriage. I started talking with a woman at the recruiting station, who had just enlisted in the Navy herself, and we hit it off. We kept in touch, even when I had to return back to where I was assigned, and the next time I went back home to Indiana, we decided to get married. We both ended up getting stationed in Norfolk, Virginia, where I was stationed on the USS Oklahoma City SSM723. I was assigned there for my remaining five years – while my second wife was stationed at the nearby Oceana Naval Air Base during the rest of her four year hitch. We had the two girls from my first marriage living with us, and we had another beautiful daughter of our own, Taylor.

Also during that time, I was deployed as part of the Gulf War action in the 1990's. Unfortunately, I won't be able to tell you anything about that until 2039. That's because in 1989, I signed an agreement that, for 50 years, I would not disclose where our sub was sent and what we did once we got there.

What I can tell you is that we drilled constantly during that time period. These would be simulations where we would have to deal with what happened if we lost power, if we flooded, or any other similar difficult situation. Strangely enough, that helped me later after I lost my sight – because many of these drills assumed we had no light, so we'd be running around in the dark trying to carry out our duties.

The most danger I personally faced on the sub was when I was cleaning underneath our main lube oil sump in the frame bay. All of a sudden, because of where we were situated, the sub had to dive or we would have been spotted. Now, I was next to the hull of the sub, as I mentioned. Located by that shell are the beams that make up the skeletal structure of the sub – and when the sub dives, the space between the sub frame and the sump compresses dramatically – which meant I had to quickly roll between the beams, in what's called the frame bay, or get instantly crushed. I was safe for the moment – but the compressed space also meant I couldn't get out!

I was trapped there for many hours, so long that I ended up eating two meals where I was trapped. I guess it could have been worse, they could have given me potatoes and peanut butter, but I still felt like a sardine trapped in a can. They did their best to improve my situation, shoving some blankets and pillows down to me so I could be as comfortable as possible and, more importantly, so I wouldn't get hypothermia from the chill of the hull. The sub captain came back and promised me they'd let me out when they could – but nobody was sure how long that would be. After being there for so many hours, I was getting a little worried, although I had to be happy that my bladder hadn't threatened to bust.

Finally, the captain sent word back. He said, "Tell Lonnie to be ready. We've got a little window where he can get out. But he's got to be ready to move fast." Believe me, I was. The sub climbed up in the water, I quickly crawled out of my crawlspace, and the sub just as quickly dove back down. I was lucky. If the captain hadn't found that opportunity, I could have been trapped there for days - which would have meant using a bottle for any bathroom breaks.

That was the one instance where I was the only one in trouble on the sub. There was another occasion where practically everyone else was. 1991's "Perfect Storm" was a nor'easter that got together with Hurricane Grace and became a whole new hurricane that the <u>National Hurricane Center</u> left unnamed to avoid confusion. Its destruction was enormous; damage totaled over $200 million and 13 people were killed. It is, of course, most famous for having inspired *The Perfect Storm* movie starring George Clooney and Mark Wahlberg.

I wish sitting in a theatre watching that film had been my only experience with this massive storm - but our sub got caught in the middle of it. We couldn't dive deep enough to get out of the cycle of waves it left in its wake, so we had to ride the storm out; it was the only time I remember that we couldn't completely escape what was going on above the surface. Instead, we were rocking and rolling so much that at one point I had a throttle man, a reactor operator, and electrical operator sitting in front of me who all just leaned over and lost their lunches at the same time. I had been always one of the first to get sick to my stomach, but never one to actually throw up – and even the Perfect Storm didn't change that fact. I offered to stay on watch, because nobody else was in good enough shape to handle that duty.

I really enjoyed my time in the service – I even made Sailor of the Year on the sub in 1993, which meant I got to go to Oklahoma City (as I mentioned, our sub was named for that city), get a personal tour, and be awarded the key to the city. Unfortunately, I never found anything it actually unlocked.

At the same time, being in the Navy had a big downside – I didn't see my family enough because of all my deployments. Now, after nine years of service, I faced a big decision. Generally, people who go 10 years tend to stay for 20. So – should I stay where I felt comfortable and knew I had a secure future? Or should I leave the Navy and make sure my family wouldn't forget my name?

It was a tough call, and yet, it wasn't. My family had to come first.

And, to be honest, home was where my heart was. One time near the end, I was able to come home to Indiana on leave. I went with my dad to the river where we had fished all my life. We made ourselves comfortable at a favorite spot and I just kept casting, fishing and reeling the line back in, over and over. My dad finally looked over at me and said, "Hey Lonnie, you realize you don't have any bait on that hook?"

I said, "Yep, but ain't that oak tree over there awfully beautiful?"

I could not have cared less whether I caught a fish or not. I was just glad to be back home.

It was where I belonged.

Chapter Three

The Accident

The worst day of your life can start out just the same as the best day of your life. You just never know.

It was the 4th of May, 1997. I was up before the sun and my friend Tim had just pulled up in my driveway. It was the typical beginning to a typical day of hunting for me and Tim – with absolutely no sign that both of our lives would be changed forever in just a few hours.

Three years earlier to the day, I had left the Navy for good. But it wasn't the end of my service. When I returned home to Indiana, I joined up with the Army National Guard, the 2nd-150th field artillery unit. That, of course, was not a full-time job, but I managed to secure one of those as well.

A new power plant, a coal gasification plant, was being built in Terre Haute and I was hired on as an operator. I had to work a lot of hours since the plant was being constructed from scratch and a great deal had to get done in order to get it completed and online. It was also a 40 mile drive from home - so I was still away from home a lot. Despite that, my wife and I settled into pretty much a normal family life. We got a little house and our girls, who were 2, 6 and 8 years old when I got out of the service, were able to enjoy the kind of childhood I had experienced as a boy.

However, three years later, any ideas I had about a so-called "normal" life were gone for a good in a split-second of extremely bad luck.

The funny thing was, that split-second, as far as I can determine, happened within minutes of that third anniversary of me walking off a naval base for the last time. At the very least, I guarantee it was within the same hour. I leave it to others to guess what that means, if anything.

Anyway, as I said, that Sunday morning was nothing unusual - we were going hunting, as we had thousands of times before. Well, Tim was going hunting; I wasn't even bringing my gun. The day before, he had taken me turkey hunting for the first time and dang if I didn't bag a bird. Now, he wanted to go back and get one for himself.

Tim Hale and I had been friends since we were literally in diapers. We grew up together; we were always in the same class in school and I considered him to be one of my closest friends. We went hunting, fishing, and trapping, and we also had a good time just goofing around. We understood each other and enjoyed hanging out together. As a matter of fact, we were roommates in college for a year, and we both signed up with the Navy at the same time.

But while I pursued submarine duty, he went to nursing school for four years, after which he became a corpsman attached to a Marines unit. He left the Navy before I did, and came back to Indiana, where he got a job as an emergency room nurse at a local hospital. When I moved back with my family a few years later, we started hanging out and doing things together again as if we'd never stopped. Even after that horrible day, I still feel that Tim is a really good guy and a good friend – I don't know how else to put it – and to this day, he remains an important person in my life.

That morning we jumped in my truck and headed out to where we liked to hunt turkey. We parked near the woods and walked in around a mile towards the same area where I had harvested my gobbler the day before. The sun was up now, but still very low in the sky.

> Tim Hale: *We went up this stripper hill – that's what we call it when they dig a coal mine in the hill and then leave it. I put Lonnie on the back of the hill, down from me about 80 yards, and I went down the front, down a gradual slope. For about a half hour or so, I was doing turkey calls. I had seen a turkey down the hill from me and I didn't know where it had gone to. It was a good distance away and looked like it had gone off towards the top of the hill. I turned around as slow as I could so the turkey couldn't hear me. I kept my focus up the hill, thinking to myself, 'If I see that white or red turkey head, I'm going to blast him.'*
>
> *Unfortunately, Lonnie had a face mask that had white and red blotches on it, along with a few other colors – and he came crawling into the spot where I thought the turkey had gone. I'd seen the head up there and I had my sights on that location.*

I was in an area that was very thick and dense – where the big birds liked to hide. Suddenly, everything seemed to come to a standstill all around me.

I remember moving through the brush and suddenly, there was complete silence. I couldn't hear the leaves rustling, I couldn't hear the birds singing. It was as if time had stopped.

And suddenly I felt a presence.

Whatever that presence was all about, it gave me a weird feeling – like it was trying to warn me about something.

For no real reason besides that feeling, I started to raise my hands up towards my face and, at the same time, crouch down and duck, because I knew something wasn't right.

But I didn't get it done in time.

I was about nine steps away from Tim when he shot me full-on straight in the face with his shotgun.

Tim didn't see me any more than I saw him. He just thought I was game – and I had no idea he was there at all. Because I was half-crouched, the impact knocked me over – I'm not sure if I completely flipped over or what, but I ended up on my stomach. I managed to get back up on my knees, and I remember thinking, "Man, I've got crap in my eyes."

I had no idea how injured I really was. I tried to wipe my eyes clean with my hands once, then twice – and then it dawned on me…

I couldn't see anything at all.

Everything was totally black.

I dropped my head. Even though it had only been a few seconds, I was already wondering to myself if I would ever be able to live normally again, whether I would be capable of doing the things I loved to do, living the way I wanted to live.

What I was already asking myself was whether that split-second had destroyed the rest of my life.

I heard Tim come running over. He said a few things quickly, but I don't remember what the words were. He was so upset he probably wasn't making much sense. I felt him pick me up, throw me over his shoulder (it wasn't hard for him to do that – remember, I'm a little guy) and start walking through the woods. I knew this was not a good move, but

Tim, panicked and worried about me, wanted to get me to a hospital ASAP.

"What are you doing, man?" I said.

"I'm going to carry you out of here."

"You can't carry me out of here; you've got to put me down!"

"I've got to carry you," Tim replied. "If I don't, you'll be dead before I get back."

"The only chance I've got is for you to put me down. Otherwise, I'll be dead before you get me out of here."

He realized I was right. We were pretty far into the woods and he needed to go get help fast. If I was weighing him down, that wasn't going to happen.

> Tim Hale: *I cleared his mouth - he had a lot of blood in there. I also told him to stay on his side, because if he tried to turn over, he could choke to death on his own blood. He was bleeding a lot - I really thought he was going to die. Because of my medical background in the military, I knew there was nothing I could do with that type of wound out there with nothing on me – I just needed to go get help.*
>
> *I'm sure it was the worst day of my life.*

We talked a little bit and I finally told Tim, "If I don't make it, tell my girls I love them." Then he took off as fast as he could.

Now all I had to do was stay alive until he came back with help.

I could only imagine the horror show that was now my face. I could feel the shotgun pellets everywhere. I also knew I was losing a lot of blood and that it was critical that I keep my head above my feet. Fumbling around on the ground, I used my hands to make something of a pillow with the dead leaves that were scattered around where I was laying.

When that was done, I laid my head down on the bed of leaves and started visualizing my kids' faces. I knew my sight was gone, most likely for good, and I never wanted to forget what my girls looked like, never. That's why I put all my mental energy to work for a few moments burning those beloved faces into my memory for good.

My next instinct was to say a prayer - a prayer to just let me live until I got my children raised, until they were all grown up. I prayed like this because I had a cousin whose husband was killed in a head-on collision a few years earlier, leaving her kids with no father. I saw firsthand the difficulties they had to go through because of that traumatic loss, and I didn't want my wife and kids to go through anything like that. So I asked God to please, just let me make it through this.

I left what I could in His hands…but I knew I had to do my part now. I had to get back to the business of staying alive.

That was getting extremely difficult. So much blood was coming out of me that it was starting to clot and block up my throat. That meant if I passed out, I would literally drown in my own blood. With one of my fingers, I kept trying to dig the thick liquid out of my throat so I could catch a breath and stay conscious.

That didn't work for long. I got to the point where my finger couldn't get in deep enough, so I felt around and discovered a little bush that was nearby. I broke off a twig from it and I began to stick it down my throat, so I could clear enough of a passageway for air. It was not pleasant, but I wasn't thinking about pleasant; I was thinking about survival.

It helped, and after a couple jabs, I was able to breathe well enough so that I wouldn't go under.

Then it was a matter of waiting. And waiting. And waiting.

Finally, after who knows how long, I heard the sirens in the distance. I heard those sirens stop and then, a few minutes later, I heard people walking towards me. My heart soared. Help was on the way.

And then I heard those people walk *past* me.

Again, the woods were so thick where I was that it was hard for them to spot just where I was. I couldn't do much when it came to helping them find me. By that time, I was so weak, I couldn't get up on my own power to show them where I was. I couldn't even yell. I tried, but all that came out, according to one of the guys looking for me, was something that sounded like the whimper of a sad puppy.

The one who finally found me was a big guy by the name of Lonnie Todd, but we all call him Pooch. He was, like Tim, another great lifelong friend. When he came across me, he was certain that I was dead, no question in his mind. My green camo hunting outfit was completely soaked with blood, front and back, top and bottom, everywhere. "How could anybody live through that?" he wondered to himself.

He quickly hollered to gather the rest of the search party - which I discovered included my dad. I also later found out that he insisted on being part of it and wasn't going to take no for an answer.

Lonnie's Mom: *Jerry and I were at home when a car pulled up in the driveway. We were told, 'There's been an accident; Lonnie's been shot.' We didn't know any other details. We hurried out to meet the ambulance, which was parked by the lake across from the hill where Lonnie was. They were about to go on the boat to go look for Lonnie.*

Lonnie's Dad: *They wouldn't let me in the boat with Lonnie – they said I couldn't go. I said, "I'll tell you guys something right now. That's my blood bleeding over there in them hills, and I'm going to go one way or the other. If I have to swim the lake or whatever I've got to do, you guys ain't stopping me from going, I'll tell you that much."*

The medical personnel put me on a stretcher and carried me over the hills to that lake, where the boat was waiting to take me across to the parked ambulance.

Lonnie's Dad: *It was not easy, I'll tell you. We had him in the boat, and the paramedics came in and we took the bandages off of his face. Immediately, I could see that his eyes were shot out. Not a very pleasant scene. He was drowning in his own blood, is what he was doing. It's hard to talk about. If you sat in a boat with your son and you don't know if whether he's going to live or if he's going to die - it's not an easy thing to talk about.*

I knew my dad had to be in a state about my condition. Even though I couldn't see, even though I couldn't talk, I felt I needed a way to reassure him as we rode across the lake on the boat.

As you might recall, my dad had the infamous nickname of "Birdie," due to his willingness to flip somebody off at the drop of a hat. Well, I knew, as I was lying in that boat, that my father had to be torn up inside wondering whether I was gone for good, just as Pooch had wondered. That's why I used what little energy I had left at that moment to do something that might have struck onlookers as a little unusual – yes, I gave my beloved daddy the finger, so he could see I knew he was there, I knew who he was, and I was still thinking right.

> Lonnie's Dad: *Yep, he sure did. He let me know that he was okay. I knew exactly what he was doing. When you have a bond like that with your son, and my wife and I both have it actually with both my sons – to have a bond like we have, money doesn't buy it.*

They took me off the boat and put me in the ambulance. The ambulance raced to a local baseball diamond, where an emergency helicopter was waiting for me. As the helicopter flew off to the hospital in Indianapolis, about 80 miles away, the medical personnel put a tube in my throat so I could breath. It worked a lot better than that stick did.

It had to have been at least an hour and a half from the time of the accident to my finally receiving treatment in the hospital's emergency room. There, the first order of business was to stop the bleeding. As the doctor told me later on, "I don't know how you made it. You lost so much blood. Fifteen more minutes and you wouldn't have made it."

Frankly, everybody had assumed I wouldn't survive, and that included my dad. After he put me on the helicopter, he went to get my mom and, in his mind the whole time, he was thinking to himself, "I'm just going to end up picking up his corpse."

I think what saved me was the fact that I didn't give up right after I had been shot. I didn't just lay down and let myself go under. Instead, I kept myself conscious, and I did what I needed to in order to keep on breathing. But I was also lucky. I could have easily bled to death if help hadn't gotten there in the nick of time.

After just one day in the hospital, I was already talking and joking with whoever came in to see me. And, because I was and am so blessed, there were a LOT of people coming through my hospital door. I had so many family and friends visiting, both from the area and all over the country, the hospital had to take one of their recovery rooms and turn it over to my concerned crowd. I had a total of 70 to 80 visitors and that was the only way the hospital staff could handle that big a group.

Of course, it helps your mental state tremendously when you have that kind of show of support from those you love and care about. They made me feel incredibly well looked after, and that, in turn, boosted my spirits high into the sky. Maybe too high, because I was acting like nothing had happened to me – and when I did acknowledge it, I laughed and joked about my injuries with everybody who came into my room. I was on a pure adrenaline high and most likely still in a bit of a state of shock – I wasn't really feeling physically what had happened to me yet. I was acting like I felt so good, that, on day three, the doctors said I was ready to go home – even though the nurses all felt I was being released too soon.

Turned out the nurses were right.

After I was home for only about a day and a half, my body completely crashed – and I headed right back to the hospital, where I would spend almost two more weeks recovering. It was a harsh reality check - my body had suffered huge physical trauma and it finally just quit on me. The first X-rays showed that there were at least 85 shotgun pellets inside of me. Tim's scattergun got me so badly, I was told you couldn't point your finger directly at any part of my face without tagging at least two pellet holes that had been put in it.

Apparently, there's a good way to get shot in the face and a bad way. I was fortunate in that I got shot the good way, if there's a way you can add good luck to that kind of situation. Because Tim had shot at me straight on, the pellets went in me the same way - no ripping or tearing of my skin or muscles, and no visible scarring, except for the holes that would eventually heal up. Even today, people look at me and tell me that they would never know I had been shot in the face if they didn't already know (of course, they could be lying to me, how would I know? You can look at pictures of me and decide for yourself!).

Nevertheless, I still had to have surgery on my nose, neck, throat and eyes, so the doctors could remove as many pellets as they could find and repair any damage that had occurred. Also, there was the matter of my two missing teeth from the blast (I was lucky that was all I lost, because I still have pellet fragments down three of my gum lines – I can feel them with my tongue today).

And, finally, an eye specialist confirmed what I already knew – I would never see again.

I was lights-out blind for good.

Chapter Four

Bug

Coming home the second time from the hospital meant a very tough period of adjustment. And not just for me.

First, there were my daughters. Children, of course, love and depend on their parents and when something severe happens to one of them, they can't help but react at a very deep emotional level.

When I was originally taken to the hospital after the accident, my girls were brought over to my aunt's house without being told much about what had happened to me. My youngest girl, Taylor, whom I call "Bug," was 4 going on 5 at the time and only knew that whatever was going on was plenty serious.

Bug: *We were getting ready for church – it was my mom and my two sisters and we were all in the house. Our friend Sue knocked on the door, and she said to my mom, "Stop getting ready for church. You need to come with me, and we need to get the girls, and there's been a hunting accident. Lonnie is involved." Mom broke down and my oldest sister, Courtney, who was 11 at the time, kinda freaked out, because she was old enough to know what might have happened. Ashley was panicked too. For me, it was about everybody else - I could feel people's emotions more than my own. I was panicked and worried because everyone else was.*

When I did finally come home, it was hard on my girls to see their father in the condition I was in. They cried, but I just gave them a hug and told them that daddy was fine and I was going to be all right.

My condition was also, of course, very hard on my wife; she had to handle everything around the house, inside and out. I was of no help, because I was now in a tremendous amount of pain, and not just because of my eyes. I also suffered from excruciating headaches that just kept coming and coming and getting worse and worse. When it was finally necessary to take me back to the hospital for the second time, every bump in the road on the way caused me searing pain in my skull, even though the ambulance was just creeping along to minimize my discomfort.

The doctors kept trying to find a way to get rid of the pain but nothing seemed to be working. To add to my misery, my body was also still incredibly weak. I ended up losing forty-nine pounds even though I was drinking Ensure shakes like they were water. I just couldn't keep weight on; I didn't even know why, except maybe my body was working overtime to heal.

So I felt very, very fragile. Fun-loving talkative Lonnie was in hiding - I just wanted complete silence at home, and that meant no more visitors. As a matter of fact, a sign was put in our yard that basically said that I appreciated everyone's concern, but I really couldn't deal with anybody coming over at this time.

There was, however, one person I did need to talk with, because he was the one who just might have been having the hardest time of anyone, including me – and that was Tim.

> Tim Hale: *I think I went through more of a depression than Lonnie did. He may have been that down, but he never showed it.*

Tim was struggling mightily with the guilt over what had happened to me. It had been his finger on the trigger, so he naturally felt entirely responsible for my blindness and pain, and that was an impossibly huge weight to carry around.

I did my best to relieve him of it.

I said, "Tim, you didn't do this. It might have been your physical hand, but, in my opinion, Satan pulled that trigger trying to separate us, trying to create a bunch of trouble. I know in my heart you never would have done anything to hurt me. I *know* that. You owe me nothing except one thing: always be my friend. Let it go. I know you can't right now, but do your best to try and let it go."

He accepted what I said, and I hope it brought him a measure of relief, because I meant every word of it. I never had a second of resentment toward him. I can also say, with all honesty, I never, ever have felt one iota of anger or bitterness towards him. And that, to me, has been a gift. If I had to carry all those dark emotions around, all they would have done is injure me further. They would have eaten me up and torn me down.

That's not what I'm all about.

At first, however, I did certainly feel down and out. The first couple of months of my recovery at home were very difficult, both mentally and physically. The pounding headaches wouldn't go away, and I was growing more and more frustrated with myself. I kept thinking that I would no longer be able to do the things I normally would do, the things I enjoyed. Nor could I take proper care of my wife and kids. I felt helpless, and that's an emotion that doesn't sit well with me. When you're used to doing for yourself all your life and all of a sudden, you feel that's taken away, you suddenly don't feel like much of a man.

Much of that helpless feeling was caused by my physical condition. I did need time to recover. At the same time, however, I was also held down by fear, the same fear I experienced in the first seconds after I was shot, the fear that I would never have a normal life again, even if I survived the shotgun blast. Everyone around me just magnified my fear. They were loving and well-meaning by constantly doing what they could to compensate for my blindness, but they were also making me feel even more powerless. They were quick to tell me what I couldn't do by myself – and quick to do it for me so I wouldn't even try.

Still, me being me, I was restless. I had to try something. One day, after two or three months at home, I had had it. I grabbed a broomstick and managed to walk outside and find my way from my house out to the barn, using the broomstick to guide myself around obstacles and make sure I didn't walk the wrong way. The total distance was only a couple hundred feet, but the thing that I noticed immediately was that the weeds were really overgrown – I could feel them reaching all the way up to my chest.

The yard was something I never would have let go before the accident. For some reason, that really upset me. This dumb little thing – just getting the weeds mowed down – was something that in the past I would have just done in a few minutes without a second thought. Now, without my eyes, it seemed like a huge, hopeless task that I would never be able to accomplish in a million years.

Helpless. That's what I was. And that's how I felt as I found my way back to the house with that same broomstick.

I didn't know it, but Bug was watching me the whole way. She didn't know it, but she was about to save my life.

As I mentioned earlier, "Bug" was my nickname for my youngest, Taylor - each one of my girls has a nickname - I call Courtney "Court" and Ashley, "Peanut". Anyway, like I said, Bug had been watching me, because this was the first time I had tried the walk to the barn since I had been home. I recognized her cute little voice as she said from the porch, "Daddy, what's wrong?"

I wasn't sure what she meant, so I said, "Nothing, Bug."

She wouldn't let it go. She knew her daddy, all right. "Yeah, there is. What's wrong?"

I chuckled, I couldn't help it. I couldn't get one past her.

"Well, if you've got to know, Bug, I'm just a bit frustrated."

I heard her stomp her foot on the ground and I could suddenly visualize crystal-clear what she was doing. I remembered when she would get feisty, she would always take her little right hand and point it up at me while she kept her left hand on her hip. I was sure that was exactly what she was doing now. The memory made me smile even as her voice got even more serious.

"Daddy, *why* are you frustrated?"

There was no way around it; I was getting called out by a five-year-old.

"Well, Bug, I can't get into my barn with chest-high weeds and I can't mow the weeds because I can't see!"

She said, quickly and simply, "Well, Daddy, I'll help you."

I said, *"What?"*

"I'll help you."

I had to think about that a moment. But just a moment. She had just flipped a switch in my brain. What the heck. Why couldn't I do it?

"Okay, Bug, if you've got the guts, then let's try it."

And with that, she led me over to the garage, where I lifted up the big door and took a big breath.

"Now, take me to the lawnmower."

She did as I asked. The riding mower was the lone vehicle in the garage and, luckily, it was facing out the way I wanted to be facing, towards the open door. I took another big breath, sat down on the mower, put Bug on my lap, fired it up and headed out the door.

As we got outside, Bug yelled, "Stop!"

"What?"

"The truck!"

"Where is it?" I asked.

"Right there!"

Being five, she didn't stop to think that saying "Right there" didn't do me much good. I had no idea of where "Right there" was. I asked her to point at the truck and I then felt her arm to get which direction it was in, so I knew where not to drive the mower. Then I turned the wheel, backed the mower up, turned the other way and went around where I supposed the truck to be.

This went on a couple more times. "Stop," she'd yell, "The tree!" Or "Stop! The fuel tank!"

Finally, I told her, "Bug, if we've got to go left, you start turning the wheel that direction." I pointed left and I started turning the wheel like I wanted her to. "I'll feel you. And if we've got to go the other way, start turning it that way and I'll feel you and help you."

With that system in place, we mowed right through from the garage to the barn. Once I got there, I had her get off, go back to the house and watch. I wanted to do this part on my own. I just had to figure out how to do it.

I got the broomstick I had used before and slowly got the mower close to the barn until I could put my hand on it. Then I squared up the mower, fired it up and mowed a lane around the barn by continuing to keep my hand on the side of the barn. Then I took the broomstick and used it to square up the mower next to the lane I had just cut, and mowed a second lane right next to it. And then a third one.

Finally, I was done. I shut off the mower and walked back up the house. I could hear Bug sitting there, going "Yup, yup, yup" and finally saying, "You did it, Daddy! I knew you could do it."

She knew, even though I didn't. But she had made me believe I could. I picked her up and gave her a big hug and said, "Yeah, you're right."

It was about ten minutes later when my dad pulled up in our driveway, came up to the house, and asked in confusion, "Who mowed around the barn?"

"Tell him, Bug," I said.

She told him – and he got really mad. As a matter of fact, he was furious that I had gone and done that on my own.

"I told you that if you need anything done around here, you should tell me and I'll do it, or I'll find somebody who can! You're crazy for taking that chance! What if something bad had gone down here?"

"Nah, Dad," I answered. "Do you see what just happened here?"

"Yeah," he said, "You mowed around your barn!"

"No, it's much more than that."

"What do you mean?"

I smiled. "You see that little girl right there? To that little girl and her sisters, I can still do anything in the world. Well, that's who I'm going to be again. I'm going to do my damndest to do everything I can, just like I used to."

I had no idea how far that simple statement would take me. I'm certain my father didn't either.

Maybe none of my future adventures would have happened without Bug. All three of my girls' belief in me was a big turning point. They thought I still had value. That, in turn, made me feel like I could still do things that I had thought I couldn't – things that others, even my own father, thought I couldn't.

But, to me, the true meaning behind that story was the second time the Good Lord had sent a child to save me. In both cases, I was loved and valued even though I was not perfect. I had worth.

It took 14 years for me to be able to tell this story to anyone else – because I just couldn't get through it without breaking down. When I did finally tell it, it was to someone who desperately needed to hear it. You'll hear about that later.

For the moment, I had experienced a profound revelation that I carry with me to this day: You can choose to be helpless...or you can choose to *live.*

All three of my girls - Court, Peanut and Bug - helped me to make that choice. The right choice. And I never looked back after I made it.

With my three girls, Ashley, Taylor and Courtney – or, as I call them, Peanut, Bug and the Court (2013)

Chapter Five

Back in Action

All three of my daughters had helped heal much of my spiritual pain – and, thank goodness, a medical procedure helped heal most of the physical.

As I mentioned, the headaches I experienced were extremely debilitating. They wouldn't stop and finally, I was sent to the Johns Hopkins Hospital in Baltimore for a treatment designed to stop them for good. The treatment itself, however, turned out to be a horrible ordeal.

The idea was to inject alcohol into the optic nerves behind my eyes to deaden the pain. So, literally, they had to give me shots right through my eyes. They couldn't give me any anesthetic for this particular procedure, so I had to man up and take the pain full-on. And when I say pain, I mean this treatment hurt worse than getting shot in the face.

They just sat me down in a chair and told me to hang on. My dad was in there with me, and he told me to grab his hand for support. I did. Unfortunately for him (and for me), the shots hurt so bad that I clamped onto his hand with a grip of pure iron. I was grabbing onto him with so much force that he couldn't take it anymore. He actually had to ask me to let go of him.

> Lonnie's Mom: *Jerry said, "My hand. I thought he was going to break it." I don't know how Lonnie could stand it. I get injections in my eyes now for something to do with my age – and they numb me before the shot. And every time I'm afraid about it, I think, 'If Lonnie could do what he's done, I can do this.*

It was so painful that when the doctor was actually giving me the shots in my eyes, I could feel tears dropping from her eyes into my lap and onto my hand. She obviously felt terrible about putting me through this. But it had to be done – and it all ended up being more than worth it. It was the next huge step in my recovery. The headaches stopped and, not long after that, I was able to get off all pain medication for good.

Another important step for me in terms of reclaiming my life was getting my job back at the power plant, which was now up and running. I had been going through a state-funded program called Vocational Rehab and they helped set up my workplace so I could go back to the plant and be productive. The computers were programmed so they would actually talk to me and tell me the plant readings. There was a program called Window Eyes that allowed me to monitor everything that was going on – everything was voice-activated. If I had to be blind, thank God it was at a time when technology could do so much.

So I was back at work full-time, forty hours a week. Every work day, I hitched a ride with neighbors who worked at the plant. Strictly speaking, it wasn't carpooling, because I couldn't take my turn driving. I tried to get them to let me, but they didn't think that was such a good idea!

By the way, in case you think a blind man at a power plant is about as useless as a baseball pitcher with no arms, there was at least one time that things could have gotten really ugly if I hadn't been there.

Because I had helped construct the power plant before my accident, I knew it inside and out, which gave me a great deal of insight when it came to analyzing the readings the computers gave me. One day, those readings indicated to me that something was very, very wrong. To double-check my gut instinct, I asked one of the operators to come in, sit beside me and give me some more facts I couldn't get at on my own. I also asked some of the other operators to answer some of my questions about how the plant was running. All the additional information just confirmed my worst suspicions. I believed one of the cooling lines was blocked, and we were going to overheat sooner rather than later.

By this time, the plant manager heard about what I was saying and came down to see what was going on. He was startled when I told him that we needed to shut down the plant right now. He said, no, we weren't going to do that. I said, yes we were – or he was going to take full responsibility for what happened next.

After a second of chewing *that* over, he agreed to let me do what I was going to do.

I gave everyone instructions on how to power down the plant the way it needed to be done, because, with the situation we were in, we couldn't do a normal shutdown. When we did finally get everything powered down, the plant workers discovered that only 3% of our normal cooling water was left intact. We could have faced a disaster if the blockage had been allowed to go on much longer.

Afterwards, the plant manager came up to me and said, "How the (expletive deleted) did you do that?" I said, "Well, I just listened to what these guys said was going on. They told me what they saw, and I told them what to do."

It was cool to be able to do that, despite my blindness. But all good things come to an end, and after nine months, my position had evolved to a point where I needed to make visual inspections of various parts of the plants to do the job right. Obviously, I wasn't capable of that and there wasn't another position they could find that would be right for me. So I was out of a job again, about a year after I had had the accident.

Fortunately, that year had been a significant one in terms of developing the confidence and the skills I would need to deal with my blindness.

At first, it was just a matter of my body getting strong enough to do more physical things. For example, when I first started at the power plant again, I would have to stay seated most of the time because I was still weak. Then, like a child, I basically had to relearn how I did everything so I could get comfortable with moving around on my own.

I got a lot of help from blindness experts. Someone came over to teach me how to walk with a cane to help me navigate safely. Somebody else came in to show me how to mark items around the house so I could easily identify things I needed to get. They also tried to teach me Braille – but I could never get the hang of it. Fortunately, I can get so many electronic gadgets that talk, it doesn't really matter. As a matter of fact, it was my quest to get more of those gadgets that led me to the Grand Canyon trip – but more on that later.

My family pitched in to do what they could. For example, they buried a dog fence wire out in the yard, so it would serve as an invisible boundary for me. The way it worked was there was an electronic device on my cane. When I would swing it over the buried wire, it would make a noise like a metal detector. That way I knew I was going too far. It didn't work great, but it was helpful.

The more I did, the more confidence I gained. Again, others were there to help me every step of the way.

My cousin Craig was out to our house just as I was building my strength, and he said, "Just take a little walk down the road with me." And that was the first time I had really tried to take that kind of walk off my property.

> Lonnie's Mom: *I sometimes think he's the one who helped us get through it when he lost his sight. That sounds crazy. I know he had to be down, but he usually just tried not to show that side around us.*

> Lonnie's Dad: *I'll put it to you this way: I think he handled it better than 95% of the people in the whole world would handle it.*

I still remember the first time I walked down the road all by myself. My dog Clementine (just a pet, I have never had a service dog) didn't like it one bit. She ran after me and barked, as if to say, "Hey! Hey! You're not supposed to leave! Get back home!" Then she ran back to the house and barked, in my interpretation, "Hey! Hey! Lonnie's going somewhere! Get out here and bring him back!!" She was a very smart animal and always looked out for me. If there were other people in the house with me and somebody else came over, she wouldn't make a peep. But, if I was by myself and somebody drove up, she'd come over and bark at me to let me know I had a visitor.

I know I made a joke about driving to work a little earlier, but I actually did get behind the wheel a few months after the accident. I was down in Pleasantville, visiting with my brother Larry near where our parents lived, when I asked him to do me a favor. I said, "Hey, let me drive home. I don't think my driver's license has expired yet, I'm still legal." I doubt my argument would hold up in court, but my brother was up for it. I got in the driver's seat of my truck and he helped me steer the wheel so the vehicle didn't end up as an unwelcome guest in somebody's living room.

With the help of Larry's eyes, I was doing fine with my little driving experiment. He mentioned we were passing by my cousin Lynn's house, which meant we were about halfway home.

Then, all of a sudden, Larry said, "Uh oh."

I said, "What's the matter?"

"Here comes Dad driving the other way."

"Well, just tell me when he's close and I'll wave."

"All right."

A few seconds went by and I heard Larry say, "Wave." And I did, and just kept driving down the road.

A little later, when I was home, the phone rang. It was my mom calling.

"Lonnie?" She sounded a little agitated.

"Yeah," I said.

"Oh, you're home. I knew your dad was nuts."

"What do you mean?"

"He said he saw you driving down the road."

"Oh, yeah, that was in front of Lynn's house."

"Oh my God!" she shrieked. "Lonnie, you can't do that! Oh my God!"

What I didn't know was that my brother had ducked down in the passenger seat – so all my dad saw was his blind son casually driving a truck down the road. When he got home, he said to my mom, "I know something's not right with me, Sherry. I saw Lonnie driving down the highway. I know it was him." He thought either he was crazy – or I was!

After all these years, I'd bet on both of us if I were him.

As I mentioned, my blindness also affected how people treated me. Many were unsure what to say or what to do. I did what I could to make it as easy as possible for them, but sometimes, it just plain hurt me that someone who had been close was suddenly not around.

I had two best friends outside of my family members – one of them was Tim and the other was Pooch, the guy who found me in the woods after the accident. We always harassed each other in a fun way and nobody would talk to me the way Pooch would. He would use every obscenity in the book, and I just came back at him. It was our relationship.

But suddenly, that relationship seemed to be gone and that really stung me. Pooch quit coming around the house a little while after I came home and I didn't understand why. I would call him to find out what the problem was, and I would have to just leave a voicemail, because nobody answered. The problem was, nobody ever called me back either.

I was furious, so I had somebody run me down to his house. He was outside and I went over to talk to him, just the two of us.

"Hey, what's going on?" I said. "Where've you been? Why haven't you been coming around or answering my phone calls?"

He paused. I'm sure he didn't know how to explain. Then he finally tried.

"Well, to be honest with you, Lonnie, I don't know what to do. I don't know what to say. I just don't know."

Now, remember, I'm a small guy – and Pooch was pretty huge, about 6'2" and 230 lbs. But I didn't care. I was mad and I wanted my friend back. So I just reached up, grabbed on to his shirt collar, and said, "Listen here. I'm the same person I always was - I just can't see. You're going to talk to me the same way you always talked to me. You're going to treat me the way you've always treated me. And we'll figure out the rest."

He started bawling like a baby.

I said, "You understand what I'm saying?" and he said, "Yeah."

From that day forward, we went back to the good old days of cussing each other out.

After I lost the job at the power plant, I was back to feeling a little bit frustrated and helpless. I like to keep busy and I didn't know what to do to fill my hours. There weren't any jobs nearby that I could do, and I lived in such a rural area that there wasn't any reliable public transportation to get me to any job that might be in a city.

That's when I decided to figure out how to do carpentry without eyes.

I started by learning how to do what might seem to be the easiest thing in the world – driving a nail with a hammer. I can't tell you how many times I smashed my fingers instead of the nail. My daughters, as usual, were there cheering me on. They kept bringing me different hammers, which Bug called "bangers," so I could see what worked best. Finally, I got to the point where I developed a good rhythm and could pound a nail into wood without pounding my fingers into pieces.

Then I was ready to tackle something bigger. The way I am, I naturally decided to do something huge.

The local coal mine gave me permission to tear down a couple of old houses on their land. When my wife would leave for the day, I'd walk down the road a ways to the bi-level house I decided to tear down first. I started by going up the stairs, crawling out a window onto the roof, crawling around to the side of the roof I wanted to start with, and then taking it apart piece by piece. Then I'd bring the lumber down to the ground, take out all the studs and nails and level it a bit. I'd say I ended up tearing down about 95% of that entire house completely by myself. Occasionally, somebody would stop by to shoot the breeze…but usually, they wouldn't move much more than their gums.

Lonnie's Dad: *The first time Lonnie went up on a roof, I didn't want to take him, but he wanted to do it – so we went. I told him he's got enough obstacles in front of him with his blindness - I didn't need to put any more in front of him.*

We were sitting on a hillside not too long afterwards, deer-hunting, and it was freezing, drizzling with rain. I told him, "You know, Lonnie, you can't be too smart to be doing this with me, here I am with a blind man, and we're sitting out here like two idiots." He said, "You know dad, we're having fun. Better than sitting in the house, ain't it?"

That's the way we live – that's just the way we are.

Of course, there were a few bumps in the road along the way. One time I was standing up on the roof and the joist (the horizontal support beam supporting the roof) gave way underneath me and I ended up landing on my butt on the floor beneath the roof. Another time there was a swarm of bees around me that I, of course, couldn't see – but, luckily, my dad, who was on the ground, could. He told me to get moving NOW. And yes, I stepped on a nail once, but it never broke the skin. I always felt like someone was watching over me the whole time, because I never did get seriously hurt.

Then I worked to find a way to get back one other thing that was important to me – hunting. My brother and my friends tried a few different things and ended up designing a mount to put lasers on my bow. Whoever went with me could help me aim at the game by seeing where my laser was beaming. I had a red laser for when it was a low light situation outside and a green laser for when it was sunnier. It all took a lot of trial and error, because the laser would change up when I pulled back on the bow, but my brother finally figured out the right design. My buddies actually made the mount and I've managed to harvest a few deer with this set-up.

Of course, when you're walking literally blindly through the woods, you're bound to run into some trouble. One time, Pooch was walking ahead of me and, in the middle of the path, there was a dead tree leaning across, about five inches around, directly in front of us. I only know this because I smacked right into it. Not thinking about who was following him – namely, a guy who couldn't see - Pooch had just reflexively ducked under the tree and kept going. Leaving me to walk so hard into the tree that it broke my glasses!

But Pooch got his. I hit it hard enough, and the tree was dead enough, that a piece of it broke off, fell forward and whacked him in the back of the head. He yelled in pain, turned around and said, "What the heck did you do that for?"

"What do you mean, what did I do that for?" I answered, trying to hold the pieces of my glasses together.

"You hit me in the head!" he yelled back.

"That was payback for letting me walk into it in the first place!" was my answer.

But the best hunting story happened one year after I had lost my sight. I was back out in the woods, hunting with Tim. As I said earlier, Tim had to deal with a lot of guilt over what had happened to me. If he knew I was having a hard time, he would have a hard time. And every time I made some progress in going on with my life, that made him feel a little bit lighter.

That day, he spotted a turkey that I had a shot at. So he got behind me, helped me line up a shot over my shoulder and together, we bagged the bird. Then we were out of control with happiness, just yipping and yelling and screaming with joy.

That was a big turning point for the two of us. If I had gotten that turkey with anybody else, it still would have meant a lot to me personally. But to get it with him...well, it peeled back a few layers. That was a very, very special moment to me. It seemed like the closing of a circle...and another big step in our healing.

Today, it's at the point where I can tell Tim, "If I'd have realized you were related to Dick Cheney, I'd have never gone hunting with you," and get a big laugh.

Working with the table saw. (Photo by Victor Henderson)

Yeah, I still got all my fingers. (Photo by Victor Henderson)

Doing some wiring.

Target shooting. At least, I think there's a target there.
(Photos by Victor Henderson)

Chapter Six

Single Dad

I don't know if my second marriage would have broken up if I hadn't lost my sight.

It's one of those questions that can never really be answered, but I tend to think the divorce might not have happened. A big part of our problems, to me at least, was there was so much attention focused on me because of the accident, everyone forgot about the rest of my family. My wife bore the brunt of having to help me recover without anybody really considering how she felt about how her life was turned upside down.

I do a lot of work with VA programs these days and I always tell them not to make those programs just about the veterans themselves; find a way to also include their families - and include them in a substantial way. I say, "You lose your life, you lose your wife. You lose your wife, you lose your life." In other words, when something traumatic happens to you, that something can come directly between you and your spouse. You might lose your whole family, and, once you lose them, you can go on to lose your whole purpose of being. I've seen it happen so many times with other disabled vets.

My wife wasn't the only one shaken up by what happened to me. Our kids had their own adjustment to make to my new circumstances. Court, the oldest, was the most affected. Being more mature, she could sense the biggest change in both me and our family dynamics. She would also get the most worried about me when I would try one of my new adventures. Peanut, the middle one, was more cautious but also supportive of me doing everything I could – it was "Go have fun, but be careful too." And Bug, the youngest, as you've read, was all for me going for it, whatever I wanted to do. She had infinite faith in what I could accomplish – which really helped spur me on.

The kids stuck with me, but my wife grew more and more distant. I was helping put her through college when the accident happened. She ended up getting her degree and then a job, but she still had a large burden to carry in terms of taking care of so much that I could no longer do. My mom tried to help out as much as possible in terms of watching the kids and doing other stuff around the house, but, my life was not the only one that had become more difficult, no question about it.

Yes, I did what I could, but it wasn't enough for her – until finally, it ended up being very clear that she was on her way out the door. But I kept trying. For example, she wanted a little add-on put on the house, so I took the lumber from one of the homes I had torn down and started to work on it. I did most of the framing myself, as well as the wiring and hanging some of the drywall and sheeting. Since I was still learning how to accomplish all that without the benefit of sight, it took me a year and a half (nowadays, it would take me about four months at most).

When that add-on was finally done, so was she for whatever reason.

The split happened about four years after the accident. Since the two oldest girls weren't biologically hers, they stayed with me. However, she got custody of Bug and that was a loss. I made sure I used every minute of visitation time allotted to me to spend time with her. A few years later, Bug did end up leaving her mom and coming back to live with me, which made me a happy daddy.

For now, however, I was a blind single parent to two teenage girls. A lot to handle even if you do have your sight, but I wasn't complaining. It was very important for me to have my daughters with me. I don't care what I end up accomplishing in this lifetime, my greatest accomplishment will be the fact that all three of my girls, when they see me, will run up to me, put their arms around me and tell me they love me.

Still, there was no question that this divorce threw my girls for a loop, and it was at this point that I decided to make a vow: I wasn't going to get married again or even live with anybody until all three girls graduated from high school. I just didn't want to get into any step-parenting issues; it wouldn't be good for them after all they'd been through. There had already been a little bit of it in the second marriage, those times when my wife would say, "They're not my kids, I don't know what to do with them." And I don't believe there's any way around it; it's a pretty normal circumstance when you remarry and you already have kids. Still, I wanted to finish raising them the way *I* wanted to raise them and not put them in a position where they had to adjust to another mother or mother figure. At this point, I wanted them, as well as me, to have some much-needed stability at home. I dated some women, but that was about it.

My wife's abrupt departure kicked things up a few notches in terms of what I now needed to do for myself, as well as for my girls. Neither daughter was driving yet, so we needed help to do the simplest of things, like get groceries and get us places where we needed to be. Here again, my parents and my brother helped out a great deal. I also would walk the two-and-a-half miles up the road to town so I could get my mail, go to the bank, maybe get a meal at the restaurant, and ordinary things like that. I had a lot of local people looking out for me as I made the rounds, so I stayed out of trouble. A small town and a tight community ensures that somebody is always there for you when you need a helping hand.

I also kept doing more and more construction work, offering a helping hand to other people when *they* needed it. For example, a buddy of mine had his house burn down. I said, "We can rebuild it and you'll save money." We did just that.

Of course, when you put a blind man on a roof, at some point, he's going to have a hard landing. I finally took a big tumble about a year after my wife left me. Another friend was adding a front porch to his house, and I was up on top of his roof doing some work there. I took a step where there wasn't any more roof, fell to the ground, and broke my pelvic bone. That gave me an even bigger challenge – suddenly, I was a blind man walking with crutches!

You want sympathy, you be that guy, let me tell you.

I quickly graduated from the crutches to a walker because crutches are horrible for a blind person. With that walker, I hobbled on down the road to do my errands as I did before I fell off the roof. A neighbor saw me, came running out in tears and asked, "Can I help you?" "No," I answered, "I just have to keep squaring up my walker with the edge of the road and aim myself towards town."

Even after that fall, I wasn't going to stop working on roofs or anything else. There was no turning back for me. It was all strictly volunteer labor. I didn't charge for my time; I was just looking to keep busy.

My Aunt Donna gave me a real boost in that department.

It was 2004 and she and my uncle were having a house built. I was talking to her at my house about the construction and she told me they were currently at the point where they were having the siding done. I couldn't help but say, "Man, I wish your workers would let me help out on that house. I could totally do it."

Well, without me knowing about it, she approached Kenny and Mike, the guys who were doing the job for her and my uncle. She told them about me and how she wanted me to be part of the crew. Well, even though I wouldn't have cost them a penny, not many people want a blind guy working on their construction job. Their answer landed in the area of "Thanks, but no thanks."

The next part I didn't find out about until a year later. My aunt told them, "You don't understand. You're either going to let him come over here and help you guys or I'm going to find someone else to help finish my house."

They changed their tune real fast.

I started by cutting and hanging drywall. So I measured a piece, chopped it off and showed it to Kenny. I asked, "How's that?" and he said, "Looks like a blind man cut it." Then he realized what he said and fell all over himself apologizing for it. He was glad I had a sense of humor about myself and that made him a lot more comfortable with having me around, especially when he and Mike saw I knew what I was doing – and was eager to keep learning how to do it better.

That led to ten more years of me helping them out on similar projects. Of course, I almost didn't survive the first one. I was working on the wiring on Aunt Donna's house and I literally asked them six times if they had the power off. "Yeah," they answered each time. So old Lonnie went ahead and stuck his pliers in there to cut some wire.

ZZZZZaaaaap! The power was NOT off.

After getting shocked about five more times – yes, it took six times in all, I'm not all that smart - I finally learned my lesson. I started to just shut off the main power breaker before I was going to do wiring. Kenny or Mike would yell, "Hey, where's the power?" and I would just say, "OFF."

Meanwhile, I had to deal with the challenge of raising my teenage girls all by my lonesome. When it came to that, I had one other big disability besides being blind – I was a guy.

I had to have a few conversations with my daughters that I never expected to have to handle. I'm not an expert on female issues, but I did the best I could. Their relationships with boys weren't a whole lot of fun for me to deal with either – nor was it for the boys. One of my girls brought one home and I told him, "Did you know I put the name of my daughters' boyfriends on shotgun shells, in case they do my girls wrong? You notice how many of these shells are empty now?"

Well, I had to admire this guy, because he came up to me later and gave me a shotgun shell he had signed himself. He said, "If I do something wrong, here's the shell. You can use it."

I loved that sign of respect.

Then there was driving.

I had an old F-150, a Ford pickup, out in the driveway that was stick shift. When the girls were younger, sometimes I'd throw them in the truck and say, "Let's just drive around the field in back of the house." I would put one of them up on my lap and she'd do the steering, I'd do the clutch and the gears and we'd just motor around. They became pretty comfortable behind the wheel and, as they got bigger, they would steer and shift.

Once I thought they were good enough, I'd let them drive down the county road. There were a few times we'd end up hitting a bump in the field a little too quickly and have to dig a bit of grass out of the bumper - or they'd fly up and hit their heads on the ceiling of the truck. But still, that's how they learned to drive. If Child Protective Services had gotten wind of a blind man teaching his kids to drive, they'd have skinned me alive.

Besides driving, I also taught them how to shoot a gun, use a bow and arrow, and fish. I sat with Bug when I taught her how to hunt deer, and when she got her first buck, she looked back at me and said "Dad?" I said, "What, Bug?" She said, "I think I can say right now that I'm as happy as a possum in a slop bucket." I said knowingly, "Wonder where you got that statement from, Bug?" Because that's pretty much my favorite expression of all time.

When my girls had a school event or a sports game, I was there if there was anyway humanly possible for me to get there. I even got a pitching machine and helped them out with their softball skills. This past year, I taught Bug how to do an Eskimo Roll in a kayak – it's how you right yourself if you happen to flip over (you'll be hearing a lot more about them very shortly). I was just so excited when she got the hang of it that I said, "I can't believe I was able to teach you that."

Her answer? "Wait. This comes from the man who taught me to shoot, to hunt, to fish, to cook, to drive…"

I nodded my head.

"Yeah, I guess you're right, Bug. I guess you're right."

Chapter Seven

Reconnecting

It was time.

I had to get ready for my post-parenting life. Not that you're ever really done as a parent, but I knew my girls were of age and could do what they wanted to do at this point. They were still helping out a lot with my day-to-day life, but I didn't want them to feel obligated to stick around and continue to take care of me. I never wanted them to have to feel guilty about starting lives of their own. I wanted them to feel free and clear to enjoy their adulthood. That meant I needed to up my game yet again and become more independent.

I had already figured out a lot of stuff on my own, but, with nobody else in the house to rely on, I still needed some kind of extra help. I learned there was great new technology available to assist me, and I wanted to get my hands on it. I'm talking about stuff like a talking GPS, a scanning device that would dictate my mail and read it to me and another gadget called an ID Mate, which could scan the bar code of whatever I bought and tell me exactly what was in it. If it was something that needed to be assembled, it would tell me directions on how to put it together. Or, if it was a food product, it would tell me how to cook and prepare it. All of these gadgets sounded like small miracles to me – and who doesn't want some new miracles in their life?

Fortunately, I knew where to get these particular miracles.

In 2010, while Bug was still in her senior year of high school, I contacted the Department of Veterans Affairs to ask about their rehab program for the blind. This was my first real reach-out to the VA and they were ready to help. Later that year, after Bug had graduated, I went to the Central Blind Rehabilitation Center (CBRC for short) at the Edward Hines Jr. VA Hospital, which was located a little east of Chicago. What I didn't know was this initial interaction with the VA would be the beginning of the next and most incredible stage of my life, a stage in which I would go places I never expected to go and do things I had never dreamt I would be given the opportunity to do.

In my mind, I was there solely to get some technological help – but the real gift I ended up receiving was of the human variety. I plugged into an amazing network of really wonderful people who would launch me into the greatest adventure of my life - kayaking those 226 miles down the Colorado River.

When I arrived at the CBRC, I had already been blind for about 13 years. I had learned to do a great deal on my own, so I went in there not feeling the need for a whole lot of help. That set me apart from most of the other people coming into the rehab program, who had lost their sight much more recently and were still struggling mightily with their new reality. I didn't feel that kind of anxiousness any longer – as I said, I was strictly looking for some gadgets to help me out with my daily routine.

The center saw it differently. They insisted I stay there for six weeks to gain what they called mobility living skills and manual skills training. I said that was definitely not necessary, and I spent about a half a day proving I knew how to cook, clean and do my own laundry without anyone's help. But even though I knew the basics of how to get by, I soon discovered there was a whole wealth of methods available to me that would make my life a whole lot easier – methods I knew nothing about. The plain truth was, because I had never had any real professional training, I had no idea how much I *didn't* know about how to compensate for my blindness. So – I went ahead and did the whole six week program anyway (and still got all the gadgets I was after to begin with – including a talking tape measure which I didn't even know existed and still love to death to this day).

But, as I mentioned, the real gift of that six week stay wasn't the training or the gadgets – it was the people I met who literally changed my life. Another big difference between me and the other guys who were my age or younger was almost all of them had lost their sight in overseas combat in Afghanistan or Iraq - not while they were hunting turkey in the wilds of Indiana. I became close friends with four of them - Eric Marts, William "Murph" Murphy, Russ Nelson and A.J. Tong.

While the other three were about fifteen years or so younger than me, Eric was around my age and shared my viewpoint about moving on with your life and focusing on playing the cards you've been dealt.

Eric Marts: *I was an army infantryman, a veteran of Operation Desert Storm, the original Iraq war in 1990 as well as Operation Iraqi Freedom. I ended up with a total of twenty years in the service. In Iraq, they started the surge when I was based in Fallujah – and that turned into my longest deployment, because the fastest way to send the largest number of troops there was just to not send anybody back home.*

Our deployment ended up being 23 months long during the years of 2005 through 2007, and in my tour of duty, I experienced multiple explosions. One of them that went off beneath my Bradley tank caused a traumatic brain injury. I lost most of my vision and I had other injuries: a neck injury and a broken shoulder. I didn't want to leave my men, so I wore an eye patch and stayed in Iraq as long as I could, but my condition got worse.

I went to the rehab center the first time in 2009. At the time, I still had ten percent of my vision in one eye. I could still walk and navigate, but not well - I was legally blind. Then I lost that remaining ten percent, and, because I was already blind in the one eye, that left me completely in the dark.

So, in 2010, I went back to the blind rehab for more intense training and that's where I met Lonnie. I was still on active duty - I hadn't been discharged yet 'cause they were trying to fix me the best they can. So I still had that mentality of being in the Army and not letting anything get in my way. You just improvise or adapt. You have an obstacle and you're trained to find a way around that obstacle whether you're going over it, under it, around it, or through it – you find a way to get past your obstacle to reach your objective.

That meant I didn't take time to think about the changes that were happening to me. I just locked into getting the training so I knew what to do. It's kind of ironic; I used to blindfold my soldiers to make sure they could take apart their own personal weapons and put them back together, because you never know if you're going to have to do it in the dark. All that training paid off for me.

I found that same kind of spirit in Lonnie, so we immediately clicked together. I also found someone I could laugh with. A lot of the other patients were really struggling and some of them would come in really bitter and angry. Me, I'm not used to anything slowing me down. And neither is Lonnie.

William "Murph" Murphy was one of those men who was having a real difficult time. When I met him, he was feeling very down about his situation. He had young kids and he had no idea how he could be a real father to them anymore. He just had no idea what he was going to do with the rest of his life.

Murph: *I'm a marine. Went into the Marine Corps on July 6th, 1994. I was in for 13+ years – I was an E-7 Gunnery Sergeant when I got out. Served in Iraq from February 2006 to September 2006. I was knocked down by an RB, a roadside bomb, when I was on a vehicle recovery mission. My eyesight didn't go right away; in fact, about two weeks after returning home, I went from 20/20 to legally blind.*

By the time I met Lonnie, I had been sightless for about four years. This was my first trip to Hines – up until then, I hadn't had any experience with any other blind people. I wasn't the best man to be around. I was still pissed off, still kind of learning how to live with losing my eyesight.

But then here's this blind guy, Lonnie, who's talking about getting up on a roof and shingling... and I'm intrigued by it. Here he is, I mean, his wife left him, he's doing this stuff on his own. I know he's doing it with his parents close to home, but here's a man who's independent. I've got a wife, I've got two kids, I've got a family who loves me – so who the hell am I to bitch? This guy, who's completely blind, starts calling himself 'Lights Out Lonnie' – or sometimes, 'Limber Legs Lonnie,' because he's a dancing fool. At the Hines Center, there were other organizations that invited us out for dinner or some other function – and if they started dancing, so did Lonnie, just shaking his butt and waving his cane. I thought to myself, "This guy doesn't have a care in the world – he's awesome!" That's how the relationship started between Lonnie and me. Lonnie became my mentor. He was the one that got me out of the dark and into living again.

I was talking to him about my daughter, and how she won't let anybody else guide me when she's around... it has to be her. So Lonnie said "I've got daughters like that too..."

I remember that moment as well. It was the moment when I knew it was finally time for me to tell someone the story of the unforgettable day when Bug had motivated me to cut the grass - and completely turned my own sour attitude around. Even though that day had happened over a decade ago, I never had been able to talk about that incident without breaking down in tears, so I could never finish the story. Finally, I stopped trying at all, because it was just too personal and meant way too much to me.

Now, I knew that story might mean just as much to Murph, so I had to make it through and get the whole thing out.

I thank God I was able to do it, even though I couldn't stop all the tears. After I was done, I added, "Murph, your kids look up to you like my daughters look up to me. That's what you are to your children. You can do this – you just have to believe you can."

I am thankful he took my message to heart and found the strength to move forward.

I found out for myself how much Bug's story meant to him when he appeared on Eric's radio show, *Heroes of the Heartland*, (which currently airs in Fargo, North Dakota, where he lives - Saturday mornings at 10 am on 970 WDAY AM, just to make the plug complete!). Eric was talking to Murph when I called in to surprise him. Murph honored me by saying to the audience, "That there's the guy who taught me how to be a man even though I'm blind." Well, Murph was always very much a man – he just needed a boost at that moment in his life. Just like I needed every boost I got from my daughters over the years since my accident.

We all had a good time getting to know each other at the rehab center – maybe too good a time on certain occasions.

Eric Marts: *The practical jokes just started and kept going. Like putting Vaseline on all the doorknobs of the blind guys' rooms. Murph would fill a rubber glove up with ice cubes and stick it under somebody's pillowcase – when it started to melt, you'd put feel the cold hand of death under your head and not know who it belonged to! Then there was the saran wrap over the toilet seat routine. Everyone started getting so paranoid about the jokes that we spent a lot of time just waiting to get pranked. But the thing is, it's hard to escape when you're a blind man who's pulled a practical joke. You just hear "Tap, tap, tap," the sound of the canes hurrying down the hall away from the scene of the crime. You might as well play the old Three Stooges "Three Blind Mice" theme over it.*

But we had so much fun. Many of the people there, they weren't very good at their mobility skills and they felt much more secure staying in their rooms than trying to negotiate the outside world and get involved. Lonnie and I were different; we wanted to do things – so we got the group together and tried to lead by example. We would save up the coffee money, for example, and have a barbeque and invite everyone.

There was this one lady at the center who had never been out of her house in twenty years – since she lost her eyesight. In the beginning, she used to at least walk out to her mailbox to get the mail. But one day, she lost her way, tripped over something, fell, and injured her hip, and all she could do was lie there on the ground until somebody found her. She never left her house again.

Finally, they brought her out to the rehab center. Once they got her learning these skills, she didn't want to go home because she was having so much fun finally being able to interact with people. It's hard enough not being able to see the world around you – it can feel like a prison cell. So you have to force yourself to go and explore things. That's where Lonnie comes in, he's a special guy. He breaks through all those barriers so people flock to him.

By the way, Eric has broken a few barriers of his own, working with lawmakers in Washington D.C. to help get disabled vets more help. As a matter of fact, he, along with his service dog Deacon, were invited as Senator Heidi Heitkamp's guests to the Presidential State of the Union Address in 2014. I've been very happy to support his efforts whenever I can lend a hand.

Eric Marts: *We've shared so much personally about ourselves – getting deeper than most people ever get because of our shared experiences. We've discussed everything from our biggest joys to our darkest fears. He's one guy I feel like I can absolutely see clearly – even though, in reality, I never have.*

Connecting with other guys who were in the same boat as me was an amazing experience – and would have been more than enough if that's as far as it went. But then, sometime during my six weeks at the rehab center, I was asked a question...

"Would you like to try to go snow skiing? We've never had one of our blind vets from here try it – and we think you can handle it."

My reply? "Well, twist my arm."

I had absolutely no hesitation about taking it on. They knew I had already been doing a lot of stuff that other blind vets hadn't, like my roofing misadventures, and considered me a good guinea pig for this experiment. I was happy to serve in that role, because I love to keep doing new things. But I had no idea how significant getting into this arena would become to my life.

The skiing trip didn't start out so well. On the "bunny hill," a chairlift isn't required because it's so small of a slope. Instead, skiers get pulled to the top by a continuous motorized tow rope. Well, at the end of that rope at the top was a great big pole – and everyone neglected to inform me of its existence. That meant I didn't know to let go of the rope before it pulled me right into the pole, which smacked me on the head and sent me flying back down to the ground on my backside. Lesson learned.

From there, the instructors taught me what a wedge was, how to line up my skis and keep them in a parallel position, and they also taught me a few basic moves. Despite my encounter with the pole, I loved it. My attitude was, "Cool, that was fun. Let's do it again!"

A little later, my new brothers from the rehab center were invited by the Wounded Warrior Project and Adaptive Adventures (an organization that sponsors outdoor sports opportunities for disabled veterans) to go to the Chicago Air and Water Show to do some more of these kinds of activities. It sounded great, but there was one big problem: I wasn't invited! The Wounded Warrior Project certainly does a lot of great work for the veteran community – but it was specifically created to help veterans who were injured in combat. That left me out because, again, the only enemy I was facing when I lost my sight was a turkey.

> Murph: *Lonnie knew about the Wounded Warrior Project through other vets that he'd spoken to – but I wanted nothing to do with that kind of stuff, I just wanted to stay at home. So Lonnie called me up. He said, "Murph, I've been talking with this girl who works with the Wounded Warriors; they've got this thing going on in Chicago," and I'm like, "Man, I don't know. Are you going?" and he's like "Well, technically I'm not considered a wounded warrior." I'm like, "Well, if you can't go, then I'm not going either." He was more than just a really good friend to me at the time, Lonnie was family.*
>
> *Finally, he gave me the phone number of the woman he had been talking to. I called her and I told her, "I'll come - but Lonnie's coming with me."*

Much to my surprise, all the guys had drawn a line in the sand and said, "No, we ain't gonna go unless Lonnie goes." Finally, the Wounded Warrior Project people called me up and asked me to talk to the guys. They wanted them to be able to take advantage of this great program even if I wasn't going to be a part of it. I understood the situation and didn't want anybody to be left out because of me – why in the world would I want to get in the way of their progress? So I told them, "Guys, you go. Have a good time. Take your wives, take your families. I'm okay, this is no big deal for me."

Their answer? "No, man, no." As each of them told me, when you've served in the military, loyalty is something that sticks with you. I was torn – I wanted them to have this experience even if I couldn't. But I also felt humbled to be looked at with such high regard by my peers.

Finally, someone from the Wounded Warrior organization called me back and said, "They'll go if you go. Would you come along for the trip?" If you've read all of this book up to this part, you already know what my answer was – YES.

I broke more new ground at the event. I got to ride a tandem bicycle for the first time, and I also sailed. When it came to sailing, I had no idea what I was doing, so I started climbing all over the rigging. I wanted to get my hands on everything so I could understand how everything worked. I wasn't about to just sit there and hold the rudder; anybody could do that. I'm not the kind of guy who just goes along for the ride. I'm an independent cuss, and that's how I approach things.

The same with waterskiing. The woman in charge didn't quite trust me to do waterskiing like a sighted person would, she wanted me to use the special equipment they had on hand for blind people like me. She said, "Hey, we've got a sit-down ski you can use, or you can try this triple-bar ski set-up where somebody skis along on either side of you. That way, you're guaranteed not to get in trouble."

I said, "How about you just hand me the rope everybody else uses and let me try it?"

She was like, "No, no, no, you can't do that." I argued with her, because I knew I could handle it. I kept telling her that was how I wanted to do it. Somebody else, hearing us get into it, spoke up. "If he wants to try it, let him try it." I could tell the woman was a bit put out, but I got to use the usual set-up.

Of course, when the speedboat started up, I immediately wiped out.

But I was persistent. I asked to try it again. This time, I got to the standing position and successfully waterskied. Now, the woman really got mad. I could tell she hoped I'd wipe out again, to prove I needed their special gear. People like that, I love to prove them wrong. It's not just important for me, it's important for others like me. They shouldn't be held back if they want to try to do more.

To the Wounded Warrior Project's credit, they recognized my strong motivation to help other injured veterans and eventually named me an official peer mentor - someone who could encourage others with disabilities to try more and do more. I was thrilled to receive this invitation, which I considered to be a gift from God. I was happy to now have access to the array of adventures and opportunities this organization could provide.

When that happened, I suddenly experienced a whole new dimension to my life. It was no longer just about pushing my own personal physical envelope to find out how much I could do. Now I was blessed with the opportunity to motivate others to get past their fears and enjoy life as I had learned to do. I was also able to connect with other organizations and meet a lot of different people involved in that kind of work.

Eric Marts: *I remember when Lonnie said, 'I'm going to run this marathon'" And I go, 'I didn't know you were a runner.' And he said, 'Well, I'm not.' They would ask him to go do something and he would say, 'Okay, I got to help out.' And that's when we started doing all kinds of stuff, all through Veterans Administration organizations and other adaptive sports nonprofits.*

It didn't matter that Lonnie wasn't wounded in combat. The big thing is that somebody like Lonnie inspires

> *people so much. Once these organizations saw how he motivated other veterans who thought they couldn't have a real life, they just turned around and said, "We're going to bring Lonnie here because people follow his example."*

All of these requests was something I never expected – it was very humbling to me, but I was happy to embrace it. I was invited to events all across the country and was able to sit down and talk to others who needed to hear some encouraging words from somebody who understood their situation. It really snowballed from there. Now I get calls from veterans everywhere: Colorado, California, Florida, New Hampshire, almost every state in this great land of ours. The calls are not just to help blind individuals; I also get asked to speak to paraplegics and vets with other kinds of disabilities. I get to go to a lot of places and do a lot of things I would never have gotten to do, simply because these people made a giant sacrifice in serving their country and need my help. That's why I do what I can to give back.

I'll be honest – there are times when I'm at some of these events, sitting and talking to these young men and women, and even their spouses, their parents or other family members, where I struggle to keep it light-hearted and positive. After one of those kinds of sessions, I frequently go back to my room and bawl like a baby. But it is a genuine privilege and an honor to be a part of their lives and I always hope I've made a difference to them. Some tell me that I have and that's very humbling. It's a gift that I never deserved and one that I'm very thankful for.

I guess whatever ability I have in reaching them comes from my own personal experience. I understand how fear and frustration can build walls around you – walls that you feel are impossible to knock down. You feel trapped by your own pain and your own limitations – and you can't find any way past all that. I talk about these walls a lot. They're created by whatever is happening in your life that's giving you a hard time – it could be a disability or you could just be going through a tough time. You just feel stuck behind these walls and without any options. So you stop trying.

Then along comes someone with a vision of what's on the other side of those walls. And they want to help you get past them. Their belief in you not only creates a door in one of those walls – it also opens that door. At that point, you have to have the courage to swallow your pride, leave behind your fear and pity, and grab hold of that helping hand as it leads you through that door and towards a wonderful new life.

That's the role I love to play for those in that difficult situation – I know how much it meant when others played that role for me. Even though I made it through my own walls, I know it's my duty and obligation to go out and find whoever else is still stuck and try to lead them back out into the light.

Ironically, often it's the ones who love you the most who help keep you trapped behind those walls. They certainly don't mean to, but their good intentions end up making things worse. For example, one man I sat down and talked with recently, someone with a wife and kids, was telling me about how his father struggled with letting him do simple everyday tasks – because that dad was afraid his son would get hurt. He was more afraid for his son's safety than his son was.

I know what that feels like. I remember at the beginning, I had to confront my dad about my getting up on the roof. I told him, "Hey, let me get up there and clean the gutters out. I've done it for how many years? If you're not going to let me help, I'm out of here." He finally had to agree, but he continued to be reluctant to encourage me to do that kind of stuff. I would tell him on numerous occasions, "Dad, if you're not going to find something for me to do, I'm going home. I'm not sitting here." He would just tell me to relax and not worry about it. My answer? "No, Dad, that's not who Lonnie Bedwell was or is. I never come around and sit and watch someone else work."

That's why, when I'm trying to help others knock down their walls, I tell their friends and family to empower them as much as possible. No, you don't want your son, daughter, wife or husband, whoever the disabled person in your life happens to be, to get hurt any more. Yes, it's more reassuring to keep them safe and sound behind those walls. But you have to understand that, in the long run, it's harmful to do that. You're keeping them in a prison of sorts, where they just exist, they don't grow and develop – they don't really *live*.

But it's a hard and lengthy process to get loved ones to really understand how much rope to give someone who suddenly has to deal with a disability. It took a while with my parents – with everybody really. My parents obviously knew the risk of allowing a blind man to do construction work and they would tell me, "It's so hard to sit around and watch you take chances." But when they thought about what I needed to try and do for myself and were honest about how I needed to learn to cope with my blindness, they would say to me, "What right do I have to tell you *not* to do it?"

Lonnie's Mom: *I'm naturally proud of him. Nervous, but proud. He could have sat in the corner and not done anything – but he's going on living instead. I have to keep telling myself that when I get worried about him.*

Lonnie's Dad: *I was tearing down a house, and he went up on the roof to help tear it off. He was still married then, and I told him, "If your wife and your mother saw us up here, they would kick my butt all over." 'And how did Lonnie, the little smart aleck, answer me? "That sounds like a personal problem to me, Dad."*

Sure, I was afraid for him. But life's got to go on. You can't put him in a corner for nothing in the world, and he wouldn't want it. When I look at him, I know - life's got to go on.

For me, it's always a very clear cut choice - you can either be helpless or you can choose to live. And when it comes right down to it, for me it's not a choice. I have to *live*, no matter what.

Chapter 8

The Challenge

The first time I ever put my butt in a kayak was at the 2012 National Disabled Veterans Winter Sports Clinic, held every year in late March in Colorado. And that's where I first became aware of Team River Runner.

Team River Runner is a wonderful volunteer-run non-profit organization, which was founded in 2004 with the intention to help active duty military personnel wounded in Iraq and Afghanistan who were recovering at the Walter Reed Army Medical Center (which has since been moved and re-named the Walter Reed National Military Medical Center) in Washington D.C. I'll let Joe Mornini, executive director and co-founder of Team River Runner, tell you a little more about it:

> Joe: *I'm a boater, a kayaker. It's been an important part of my life. I got into it because I could no longer run after I had a series of surgeries on my right knee. I love the outdoors, though, so I was looking for something that would help me stay fit and give me some adventures. Well, the Washington D.C. area is the Aspen of whitewater boating, so kayaking immediately filled that slot in my life.*

One day, my kayaking buddy, Mike McCormack and I were talking about the problem of wounded veterans returning home from overseas who lacked a physical outlet. And we thought that we should take these wounded warriors and get them kayaking on white-water. They're combat vets and they still need that kind of adrenaline. We initially started off with just ampu-tees, but now we work with men and women with all kinds of disabilities. For them, paddling is a great op-portunity, even if it's only on the flat water.

We've been doing this now for over 10 years. We now have 40 chapters in the country, thousands of partici-pants each year and thousands of paddling events. We really work hard building leadership with our wounded and disabled veterans. We want to give them purpose and let them run the individual chapters whenever pos-sible. We now also work with all disabled veterans regardless of where or when they became disabled, and we also have individuals paddling with our veterans who provide instruction and mentoring.

At this 2012 Sports Clinic, Team River Runner had a set-up where you could try kayaking in a swimming pool. I de-cided to give it a go with a friend of mine, so I went to the pool and sat in the kayak. Then I was told I could win a free t-shirt if I could do an Eskimo Roll.

If you're not familiar with kayaking, an Eskimo Roll is when your kayak flips over - and you're able to right it (and yourself) back up on the water. This is an important maneuver to master when you're kayaking on whitewater, because you're able to maintain control. If you have to exit the boat and swim, you're a lot more exposed and could possibly get seriously injured or even drown. And, of course, if you're blind, the dangers are greatly magnified.

Well, I earned myself a t-shirt that day – and, more importantly, impressed the River Runner people by listening to their instructions and successfully completing a roll. Again, this was my first time in a kayak – they're not too common where I'm from in Indiana. It was fun, I won a prize and that was pretty much the end of it. Or so I thought.

Joe: *We were doing leadership clinics where chapter coordinators would nominate wounded or disabled veterans to take part in a weeklong leadership clinic. The vets would learn how to paddle and also network with other veterans. One of those programs was initiated by a wounded warrior that I knew from Walter Reed. He encouraged me to bring this leadership clinic to his home state of Montana. We did that successfully for a couple of years, then we came up with the idea of inviting some blind veterans to try whitewater kayaking for the first time. The first year we did this, one of the blind veterans who attended named it the Outta Sight Clinic and the title stuck.*

We continued to reach out into the veteran community to find blind veterans. The idea was to pair them up with another wounded warrior who could see and could help guide them with voice commands. They would paddle all week, starting in a lake, moving up to moving water and ending up on whitewater. Afterwards, we would send them home to hopefully do outreach and find more blind vets to participate. I always want as many as possible to participate. The words people hear me say on a regular basis are 'Butts in Boats' - if I have a boat without a butt in it, I'm highly upset. It means a missed opportunity for a veteran who might need it.

One of our leadership people at the Colorado clinic where Lonnie did his first Eskimo Roll thought Lonnie was a pretty special guy and that we should bring him up to the next Outta Sight Clinic. So I called Lonnie up and invited him.

And, of course, I said, "YES."

The clinic was held in July of that year, just a few months after the Winter Sports Clinic, in Livingston, Montana, by the Yellowstone River. During the clinic, I was able to kayak for three days on whitewater. They also taught us how to do a bow rescue – where, if you flip upside down in the kayak, another kayak comes alongside you so you can grab onto the front of it to flip yourself back up. I did about 30 of those. Unfortunately, they weren't teaching us the Eskimo Roll at this clinic and I didn't remember how, so I couldn't refresh my skills on that move.

I did, however, meet another important guy to my life, Leonard Sell - only nobody ever calls him Leonard; he's known as "Chip" to friends and family alike.

Chip: *I was with the army in National Guard and Army Reserves for about twenty-five years. In 2003, I was serving in Iraq when I was wounded by a shell that went off about fifteen feet from me. A lot of us got wounded from the blast. I ended up with imbedded shrapnel in my leg and my chest. Another piece went through my nose and a few more got imbedded in my scalp. I also had a mild brain injury and, same as anybody who was in a big event like that, I incurred some post-traumatic stress. I did a couple years of physical and speech therapy to get back where I think I'm running pretty good. The army and the VA – they did a pretty good job. They took care of me.*

One day, I was in D.C., out riding my bike one day, when I went by a little canal off the Potomac River.

There were a couple of guys on kayaks in there and I immediately thought to myself, "Oh man, I want to do that." I had kayaked before, but had no idea there was an opportunity to do it here.

Then I got another nice surprise. One of the guys told me, "We're a bunch of wounded and injured service members from Walter Reed. We come out here and we boat every Tuesday, Thursday and Saturday." I said, "You're kidding me." I told them my story and the guy goes 'Go talk to that one-legged man on top of the van.' I said, "Okay – that's a pretty interesting description of a person."

I walk up to the hill and, by God, there's Rob Brown, another vet that'd just been recently injured, hopping on his one good leg - he didn't have a prosthetic one or anything - on top of a fifteen-passenger van. He was balanced perfectly and handing down kayaks. I said, "The dude down there told me you'd give me a boat and a paddle." He did and the rest is history. The group was a strong one, with the same ethics, values and morals that I think I have – and they took care of each other. They were strong and a little bit independent. And just really good to other people like me – they really wanted to help.

I continued working with the Team River Runner people, so I was at the Outta Sight Clinic in Montana when Lonnie showed up. This guy made a really great impression on me. Really, he was just so determined. There were two guys on that trip that had no vision, and they were both really impressive because they never said die, never said stop. Lonnie and I worked really well together.

The whole clinic was a great experience and I was really excited about continuing to find kayaking opportunities. That's why it was so amazing that I was able to fall into one of the biggest ones around when I headed for the airport for my flight back home.

Joe Mornini was at the airport when I got there, and we ended up having a very long conversation, our very first one. After a while, once Joe got to know me a lot better, he said to me, "Man, how would you like to be the first blind veteran to run the Grand Canyon?"

My reply? "That sounds pretty cool."

In his mind, this was a goal I could work towards over a period of time. I truly don't believe either one of us thought it would happen as soon as it did – we thought it would be years down the road.

Joe: *We talked forever – and at the end of it, and we set a goal for him to be the first blind veteran to run the Colorado River through the Grand Canyon. At the time, no blind person had ever done it, veteran or non-veteran, but someone was about to attempt it, so I thought Lonnie would get beaten on that record. As I told him, he had to prove himself before I could even think about sponsoring him on that trip. I said, "Lonnie, you need to do at least 1000 Eskimo Rolls before you even call me about the Grand Canyon."*

I had thought this through from a safety standpoint and I knew being an expert at the rolls was crucial. As big and powerful as the whitewater is, it's relatively safe on the Colorado and there aren't big rocks that could hurt somebody like Lonnie. Instead, there are wave trains that are fun and frisky, but safe. If you flip over in these ginormous wave trains, you can just roll back up again and still be in your boat. Then you just have to find the voice of the person who's guiding you, get into an eddy, catch a breath and wait for the next rapid.

Joe's offer fired me up. When I have a huge goal to shoot for, I like to move on it as soon as possible.

A few months later, in October, B.J. Phillips, one of the gentlemen that I met at the Colorado Winter Sports Clinic, invited me to join him where he lived in Kentucky for a day of kayaking. I spent about four hours paddling with him on Russell Fork, a popular whitewater location. It was another great experience and this time I ended up with a lot more than a t-shirt: Some of the other people I met in Kentucky sent me home with a kayak, paddles, a helmet, everything I needed to practice on my own.

I didn't get back into a kayak, however, until February of the next year, 2013. I had been able to talk Indiana State University into developing a Team River Runner chapter of its own in Terre Haute, and an instructor by the name of Neil Fleming drilled me on the right way to do an Eskimo Roll so I made sure I had it down.

Not long after that, Joe called me with an offer. He said, "Hi Lonnie – how would you like to do the Grand Canyon this summer?" I replied, "Are you serious?" "Yeah. You can ride in a raft to just get the feel of it."

To his surprise, I turned him down.

I told Joe, "I don't want to do it in a raft. That'll scare the crap out of me." It was true. In a raft, I would have no control over what happened and no idea of what was going on. Even though I'd supposedly be safer, I knew that mentally, it would be too tough on me.

I had a better idea.

"Joe, I want to do it in a kayak."

"What?"

"I could get thrown off a raft. I want to be in a kayak where I have control."

"Remember what I said, Lonnie," Joe reminded me. "You can't do it in a kayak until you have a thousand rolls under your belt."

Well, okay.

I have a small pond on my property. And I had a kayak. As a matter of fact, I had two, since Joe had sent me one as well. So, the day after Joe called, I took one of those kayaks down to my pond and I started practicing. And practicing. And practicing. I wasn't good at it at first; I fell a bunch of times, but I'm a persistent cuss. And, at the end of the day, I called Joe back and told him, "Joe, I did 100 rolls today."

Joe was a little shocked – he didn't expect 100 rolls in one day. And he told me that even if I did ten times that amount and hit the magic number of 1000, I still needed more whitewater experience.

I was going to go ahead and get that experience.

The U.S. National Whitewater Center is located in Charlotte, North Carolina, home to the world's largest man-made whitewater river. That June, I travelled down and called another friend of mine, Kyle Thomas, who lives in Charlotte and who I had done some mountain climbing with, and we kayaked at the Whitewater Center (around the same time, I was also able to kayak down the Pidgeon and Nantahala Rivers with B.J. Phillips).

At the U.S. Whitewater Center

While at the Whitewater Center, I also happened to run into another kayaker named Pablo McCandless.

Actually, that isn't an accurate description, because Pablo is far from being "just another" kayaker. He's so good at paddling that he was in the 2008 Beijing Olympics, representing his home country of Chile. That meant when he complimented me on how well I was kayaking, I *believed* him. There was another interesting thing I found out about Pablo: He was trained in kayaking by Mr. Joe Mornini himself!

This was unbelievable – I had happened upon a world class kayaker who had a close relationship with Joe, the guy who had to decide whether I could paddle my way through the Grand Canyon. This was the kind of coincidence that, if it happened in a movie, I'd say they made it up. Instead, it was one of the luckiest moments of my life.

After I found out that Pablo knew Joe, I told Pablo about the Grand Canyon trip – and how I wanted to kayak the whole thing. And Pablo said the magic words…

"I think you can do that."

Chills went through me.

"Pablo," I said, "You've got to call up Joe and tell him what you just told me." He did and I am eternally grateful to him for making that phone call. Joe wasn't going to argue with an Olympic athlete – so he got back to me quickly. He had to, since the Grand Canyon trip wasn't all that far off. He said, "Okay, Lonnie, I'll give you a shot." Those were some beautiful words to hear.

But Joe did still have reservations about my attempt. "

Joe: *Lonnie wanted to run the whole Grand Canyon when he'd only been kayaking for a little over a year – and only every once in a while. I'll be frank – I told him I'd put him on the list for the trip, but the chances of him being able to kayak the entire 226 miles were pretty remote. He was just too new a boater. "But," I said, "Go try it out. You're a bad ass, go give it a shot man, you got a good attitude about this thing, certainly we would like you to do this. But the first time you run into serious trouble, you're getting in the raft."*

When Pablo McCandless – a great boater – vouched for Lonnie, I felt that was a good enough of a vote of confidence. I had Pablo send me an email memo to that effect, so I'd have a piece of paper in my hand when I told the board of directors about Lonnie kayaking through the Grand Canyon. I thought they'd grind me up like hamburger. They didn't - but there was silence in the room.

In the end, I knew it was safe, I knew Lonnie had time to prepare, but he probably wouldn't be running the bigger rapids. As for me, I would be training, getting ready myself to guide him down. I thought he was going to get the shit kicked out of him. I told him, both from a

> *skills standpoint and a safety standpoint, he was not going to be able to do all the rapids. But I would get him through one way or the other. I've guided on the Grand Canyon before, guided safely, so I knew I could take care of him.*

That was a nice thought. However, what Joe didn't know is he wouldn't be taking care of me.

He ended up having a whole lot of people taking care of *him* instead.

Chapter 9

Preparations

While I was waiting to be approved for the trip, Joe sent me back to Montana for some more kayaking training. It went well - but, even so, when all was said and done, I still had a lifetime total of only 14 days of whitewater training. Most kayakers who took on the Grand Canyon route had been boating for years. Still, Joe fought for me, even though the Team River Runner board wasn't all that confident about me making it all the way. Neither was Joe – he kept telling me, "Expect to walk around a lot of the rapids."

But I was stoked. My family? Not so much.

My parents and my two oldest daughters were like, "Why do you have to do this?" I had a good answer. More and more, veterans' organizations were using me to inspire and motivate other wounded warriors, to show them what they could do if they put their minds to it. If I successfully kayaked the whole Grand Canyon, that could mean a lot to those special people who had done so much for us all.

I understood their fears, however – if it were my child or my parent, I'd have been worried too. But it seemed like their anxiety might have been getting a little out of hand.

> Lonnie's Dad: *I worried, me and his mother both worried. We were outside the house, watching on a laptop a little bit of video of him doing his Eskimo Rolls – and, on the video, he had flipped over and was upside down, so that his head was underwater – and it stayed underwater for a while. My wife started yelling at the screen, "Go on, Lonnie, get up, get up!" Then she turned to us and said, "He ain't coming up!" That's when my granddaughter had to remind her, "Grammy - he's already up. He's right there inside the house!"*

In the end, the only one who really seemed fine with me doing the trip was Bug, the girl who continue to thinks her dad can do anything. "If you think you can do it, go for it," she said. "I shouldn't be the one telling you that you can't try."

Finally the day came when I got the magic phone call – it was from Joe Mornini telling me that I was definitely going on the Grand Canyon trip. Not only that, but I would be able to try it in a kayak, not a raft. That was the good news, and, yeah, it was real good news. But the bad news was that Joe wouldn't be the guy guiding me down the Colorado River. As a matter of fact, he wouldn't be going anywhere for a while.

> Joe: *And it was because of Lonnie. I was training hard for the trip and I had a health scare that turned out to be nothing more than indigestion. But the cardiologist checked me out just in case and saw something he didn't like. He said, "Well, we're going to keep an eye on that, let's take another look in six months." That's*

when I told the doctor that we probably shouldn't wait - I was cranking my heart rate up pretty high because I was getting ready to guide a blind veteran through the Grand Canyon. He gave me a look – I was doing what??? I explained the trip and that I really needed to know my heart was okay before I left. They brought me into the hospital to do what he called the gold standard of tests – and I never got out of that hospital. They estimated I had a 90% blockage in my "widow-maker" artery and I had two other blocked arteries as well. I ended up with a triple bypass operation.

In a way, Lonnie lucked out – because I was able to get him a guide who was both a veteran and a much better boater than me. Of course, I lucked out too – because I stayed alive!

That phone call was when I first heard Alex Nielson's name.

Joe told me on the phone, "I'm not going to be there, but I've got this guy Alex who's an exceptional kayaker. You might actually be better off, because I think he's a better kayaker than me."

Alex: *I had been whitewater kayaking for several years before I met Lonnie, and several years before I got involved with Team River Runner. I was in the military for five years, serving as a Corpsman, which is like a medic, and I was deployed to both Iraq and Afghanistan during those five years. We were in combat several times and I lost some guys in my platoon that were in my care, but I myself was never wounded. When I got out, I knew I wanted to start college right away. I was kind of stressed out and didn't know what to do, so, since it was the summer, I learned how to whitewater kayak. And then I really got into it.*

A couple years later, I heard about Team River Runner while I was living in the D.C. area, and I started going over after class, while I was an undergrad at University of Maryland, real close to Walter Reed Hospital. I heard they needed people to teach people to whitewater kayak, so it was a perfect match for me. I started doing that a couple times a week and I got experience working with vets who had all sorts of disabilities – but only a little bit with blind paddlers and not on whitewater or anything close to it. I got really close to Joe Mornini, who came up to me one day in 2013 and asked if I was available to do the upcoming Grand Canyon trip. Well, for a whitewater kayaker, that invitation is a godsend. You're not going to say no to that. I had never done that trip, and it's an iconic thing, not to mention difficult to get the permits for. Unfortunately, it takes a month of your life to go and do it. So, at first, my answer was no, because I was trying to get into medical school at the time.

A week later, I changed my mind and said I would do it. That's when Joe said, "We have a blind paddler who wants to go, Lonnie Bedwell." I was a little nervous about trying to get him through the rapids, but at this point, the way Joe was talking, my impression was that he would probably spend most of his time in the raft – he wouldn't actually paddle through the bigger rapids. Joe said, "We want you to guide him, help him with his kayaking skills, and we'll see how far you guys can get."

I talked to Lonnie on the phone a couple times beforehand to get an idea about his paddling experience and what he wanted to do on the trip. I was taken aback during one of those calls by the fact that he was doing hundreds of Eskimo Rolls... in his pond! That was my first moment where I thought - this guy is different. I did think it was cool that he was paddling all over, making a very concerted effort to get experience, be-

cause a lot of times you get guys in the program that want to do something but don't want to put in the time or effort to make it happen.

I'll never forget when I finally met Lonnie. I was the one designated to pick up all the wounded vets flying in from all over the country to Phoenix the day before we were going to drive up to the canyon. It was kind of a nerve-wracking experience to make sure to get all these guys who were flying in at different times. Lonnie was the last one of the day – and, at this time, he didn't have a cellphone, because he kept saying he didn't believe in them. So I've got to pick up a blind guy at the airport and no one knows where he's at, no one can get in touch with him, no one knows what he looks like. I was driving the van by the arrivals terminal, figuring out how to find him – when I saw somebody standing there with denim coveralls, a red life jacket, cowboy boots and dark sunglasses – and he had a circle of people around him that are talking to him and laughing, he was entertaining the crowd. Of course, it was Lonnie, he was very easy to pick out – that was my first impression of him. And when I met him, I was like "This guy is interesting. He's got such a positive attitude and he's so excited about everything."

Alex was slotted to be my main guide. He would paddle his kayak in front of me and guide me with voice commands. And behind me, I would be fortunate enough to have two other amazing gentlemen looking out for me. One of them was Chip Sell, who you met in the last chapter when I kayaked with him in Montana. The other one was Mike Bradley, another wounded warrior that I was about to meet for the first time.

Mike: *I spent six years in the army as a medic. After being wounded in Iraq I was retired from active duty* with a brain injury – and I also had PTSD. I was treated at Walter Reed when Team River Runner started up and I wanted nothing to do with it. I thought it was stupid and I avoided it. At the same time, my doctors were telling me, "You're extremely overweight, you need to fight your depression." But, at the time I didn't know how bad I was and how dark of a place I was in."

Then about three years ago, a friend of mine who was also a wounded warrior was coming into town - and unfortunately, my work schedule at the time and his schedule made it hard to get together. The only time I could meet up with him was at one of the River Runner pool sessions at Walter Reed. Somehow, between him and the others that were at the session, they convinced me to get into a kayak. Twenty minutes later, I was back out of it, and I said, "I hate this, it's not for me." I was uncomfortable, didn't like it. But I had met Joe Mornini while we were at the pool and there was something about Joe that intrigued me. I wanted to know more about this guy and why he was so passionate about getting more "butts in boats."

I went back to their next pool session to talk to Joe, because I wanted to pick his brain. He wasn't there, but there were two volunteers who convinced me to try the boat again. An hour later, I did my first roll and thought, "This is amazing."

I started kayaking every day and going to every single Team River Runner session. Every single day for the first year, I would work on my skills. And I set a goal with Joe, the same goal he set with Lonnie, to be on the next trip to the Grand Canyon. I worked really, really hard and I got really, really good at kayaking.

After my first year of kayaking, I looked back and realized how miserable my life had become. I never left the house, ate junk food, gained weight. I had no social circle, I had no interaction with anybody outside of

*work. But when I built up my paddling skills and start-
ed running vigorous whitewater, I really, really enjoyed
that. Then I finally got the phone call from Joe – he
said, "You are going to be one of my guys on the Grand
Canyon trip."*

*I had really prepared myself physically and mentally
for the trip so I wasn't scared. I was excited. But then I
found out Lonnie, who I had never met, was also going
to be on the trip. And since Joe wasn't going, he wanted me to help guide Lonnie. That scared me a little, I
had no idea how that was going to go. I heard nothing
but great things about Lonnie – but it's really hard to
take somebody else's word about a stranger. So, to me,
there was this unknown. I wanted to make this happen,
I wanted to make this work, I really wanted Lonnie to
be successful – but I was also kind of wondering if it
was really possible for him to do this.*

*I had kayaked with a couple of blind paddlers on the
Potomac and each of them had his own technique of
what worked for them. I didn't know what was going to
work for Lonnie and what he would want from us. A lot
of it was about questioning my own abilities. I knew I
could get myself down the river, but I hadn't prepared
myself to guide somebody like Lonnie and to have that
person completely putting their faith, trust and life in
my hands.*

*For example, one of my concerns was Joe told me Lon-
nie liked to get voice commands, that he can track
voices very well. Well, in my mind, I'm thinking, these
rapids are massive, there are sounds everywhere, it's
just like thunder – how is he going to track our commands?*

Mike was right to have that concern – because being able
to actually hear everybody could potentially be a big issue.
But we thought we had that licked – we bought some water-

proof radios with push-button controls and we were going to tape them on to our straps so we could communicate with each other. We all thought that was a solid plan – except it turned out we could hear each other's voices better than we could hear the radios, which quickly got ditched.

It was great to meet my new guides, Alex, Chip and Mike. I sat down with the three of them at the hotel and we talked out how they could best guide me. I told them straight off the bat, "The big thing is that if you guys stay calm, I'll stay calm." I strongly felt that if everybody kept their heads, everybody would react better. We just had to keep it all simple, so we all knew what to do and when to do it.

My guides seemed great, but I was a little concerned about the equipment I was given to work with. When the people who kindly outfitted us with boats and paddles brought in the stuff, I found out my kayak was an older one and not in the best shape. Then the guy handed me a paddle to use – and I knew something was wrong with it. I said something to Alex and he saw the problem right away – "Lonnie, that's a left-handed paddle." I'm a righty and that sure wasn't going to fly. We had to dig up another paddle and re-mark it.

By the way, let me explain what I mean by marking my paddle. Since I'm blind, it's hard for me to tell where I should be putting my hands on the paddle. We would take some tape and wire and place that where I should grip the paddle, so I could always feel where my hands needed to be. That was very important, because things happen fast out there on the whitewater and I would need to get my hands back in the right place quick as I could.

This all made me a little apprehensive about just what kind of set-up I was saddled with. After all, we were about to try something never done before – guiding a blind person down 226 miles of the Colorado River, all the way through the Grand Canyon for the first time ever - and I didn't want to miss my shot at making history because of a bad kayak or wrong paddle.

For my part, I had done all I could do. I even asked Joe to send me back to the Whitewater Center in Charlotte a week or so before the Grand Canyon trip. Rapids strengths are traditionally given a ranking, all the way from Class 1, basically flat-water, to Class VI, which is for hardcore experienced boaters only. The Grand Canyon trip had rapids that ran the gamut all the way from I to VI. At the Whitewater Center, I could try the Olympic Competition Channel there, a manmade whitewater river which had Class III and Class IV rapids. I knew I needed to try those advanced rapids before I did the Canyon.

It's a good thing I did. The first time I tried the Competition Channel, I got washed out of my boat – forcing me to swim the whole thing. I ended up banging up my knuckles and cracking my tailbone. I didn't tell anyone about the tailbone – I was afraid they wouldn't let me go – and it was still hurting me for the first three or four days of the canyon run.

But I couldn't let those minor injuries get in my way. I knew I had to try the channel again – and make it without swimming. I got flipped, but I successfully did a roll and quickly got back upright. I made it all the way down the Competition Channel, rolling three times without a problem - that gave me a lot more confidence.

Still, here I was trying to navigate one of the most dangerous whitewater routes in the world. I had been told over and over that it takes years to learn how to safely row a raft through Class IV, V and VI whitewater rapids, of which the Colorado River has many. I hadn't even *tried* a Class V of VI yet. Helping me would be three guides I had never worked with before and who weren't sure about how to get me through this. I also was riding in a boat I didn't completely trust. And I wouldn't be completely safe *off* the water either - I'd be camping out every night in the wild, where, we were warned, scorpions, rattlesnakes and red ants were plentiful. I wouldn't be seeing any of those coming at me before it was too late.

More than one person who *could* see had died trying to do what I was about to attempt. I had to hope I wouldn't make history as the first blind person to go that way.

Chapter 10

The Trip

On the historic trip through the Grand Canyon.
(Photo by Marc Huster)

W e spent a day in Flagstaff, Arizona going to school.

When you do the kind of trip through the Grand Canyon that our group was planning, the National Forest Service has you watch (or in my case, listen) to several videos explaining exactly what you're required to do to help maintain and preserve the area. The basic idea is that you are to have zero impact on the area. Whatever you bring in, you take out – and nothing goes on the beaches, including your pee. You either pee in the river or in a bucket which you then dump in the river (for my purposes, a big empty Gatorade jug did the trick). And when you poop, you have to do it on what's called a "groover" – basically a big old ammo can with a toilet seat on top of it (and that was not the most pleasant experience of my life). We also had to watch films explaining the dangers that lurk in the Canyon, such as the scorpions and red ants I've already mentioned.

There were 16 people, including me, taking this trip. On August 4th, we headed to Lee's Ferry, the only place for hundreds of miles where you can easily access the Colorado River going into the Canyon. There, we spent about three hours getting the four support rafts loaded with all our gear and food. Then, so we wouldn't block river access for anyone else, we floated downstream about 200 yards to set up camp for the night.

I already had some equipment concerns. At the hotel, I discovered I had been given a paddle for left-handed paddlers, and I was a righty, so I got that switched out. I also realized that the kayak's seat and foot braces needed some adjustments, so it was good I had that short trip to figure all that out.

That morning, I had talked to Joe Mornini on the phone – it would be the last time I talked to Joe until after the trip, as communication inside the Grand Canyon would be extremely limited. Not a lot of Wi-Fi going on there. Joe told me to just accept the fact that I would end up swimming through some of the rapids, but also said not to worry about it – I should just keep moving forward. I really wanted to make it all the way without that happening. The odds, however, were not in my favor, but it didn't hurt to dream. When it came down to it, this was Joe's dream too, to have someone like me complete the trip. I wanted to make both our dreams a reality.

The night before we were to set out on the river, I could hear the flow of the river from where we were camping. The next morning, I would be on that moving water. It was an awesome feeling, knowing what I was about to attempt.

During the trip, I kept an oral diary of each day's events. These will form the basis of my recollections of the journey down the river, along with additional thoughts from Chip, Mike and, most importantly, Alex - who was, more than anyone else, my "eyes' when we were on the river.

Day 1

August the 5th. Our first full day on the Colorado. We ran 12 miles.

Before we left this morning, the forestry people gave us a safety speech. Took about an hour and a half; then we got on the river, about 11:15 am. I sat down on the river and felt it moving underneath my kayak - I was just like, "Oh my..." The volume and the force. It was intimidating.

Hit the first significant rapid on our trip, the Badger Creek Rapid, and it was definitely the biggest water I've ever done. I ran it clean. I did run my kayak into Alex's kayak in the middle of it, but he just pushed me off and we went on our way. The process seemed to work really well with Alex out in front of me, giving me directions.

Alex and me taking a break.

Alex: *The first time I actually paddled with Lonnie was that first day we were on the Colorado River in the Grand Canyon. We were paddling great all day, going through warm-up rapids and Lonnie was doing awesome, right behind me. He never rolled over and looked really, really relaxed. I was really excited about how good he was doing. And we had our first real conversation about how things were going to go. I told him, "We're going to play it by ear. We're going to see how things are working out and what we're comfortable with - but we need to get to know each other and build some camaraderie these next couple days." That's how we figured out what commands we were going to use and how we were going to navigate when the rapids got really loud. We tried out a couple different techniques and we decided to have me lead in front of him with the verbal calls, rather than have two people behind him using voice commands - or use the radios, all these other complicated things that didn't seem to work.*

Alex and I kept the commands simple, we just fed and learned off of each other. He had to learn my timing on paddling and how quick I could react to him, so he would know when to call the commands – just kind of a timing thing.

We're camping just above a rapid. In the morning, it's no more than get on the river and go "boom" through another couple of rapids that lead up to the first big one, House Rock Rapid. I'm thinking about my family back home, my girls and everything. I can only imagine Bug saying, "Yep. Go for it, dad. Go for it." It's pretty cool.

I keep sitting here thinking, man, a few years back, kayaking just wasn't even a thought of mine, let alone kayaking in the Grand Canyon. It's funny how life just throws things at you like that.

I ended up talking to Pete Winn a little bit tonight. Pete is a retired Forest Ranger who worked in the Grand Canyon for many years – his daughter, Carmen, is serving as the group's primary guide down the river. Her nickname for me is Mr. Sunshine. Pete had been on many of these trips and was there to help mentor Carmen this time around – as far as he was concerned, this would be his last ride down the Colorado through the Canyon. So he had plenty of experience. When he gave me some good feedback on how I was handling my kayak this first day, his words carried a lot of weight with me. I felt I had earned his respect already and that gave me more confidence.

But I was still worried about what was ahead – a series of smaller rapids, followed by the first major rapid we would be facing on the trip, the House Rock Rapid.

I said to Pete, "I just don't know about doing rolls in the rapids, that's the biggest thing I'm worried about." Pete said without hesitation, "Lonnie, you get out there tomorrow and you intentionally flip upside down in the first rapid, before we get to House Rock." I replied I wasn't sure about doing that, I would have to think it over.

Pete pressed on. "You don't think you're not going to flip over at all in these rapids? You don't think you're going to need to do a roll?" Well, yes, I knew I would, but I didn't know if I wanted to do it on purpose in the middle of a rapid!

Alex: *That night, we camped right above the House Rock – we could hear it all night long. I went down and I looked at it. Once you've been kayaking for a while, you can understand certain things - House Rock was big and powerful, but it's what we call forgiving as well. It might be a big, powerful wave, but if it hit Lonnie and knocked him over, he would be in a place where he could easily be rescued by us. It's hard to get into real, serious trouble in House Rock. As long as you're in the right area, it'll work out.*

So I talked to Lonnie about it. We made a pretty quick decision about it: for me, it was mostly a test of how well he could do. Lonnie was willing to take it on, even after I explained how big it was going to feel to him. But no matter how much I explained, it was still an unknown and we didn't know how it would work out for us. And we knew that if it went bad at House Rock, Lonnie was going to end up in the raft for most of the rest of the trip. There were already others on the trip that wanted Lonnie on the raft when we got to House Rock, who were nervous about Lonnie doing this. But Lonnie and I – we were determined to run it on our kayaks.

Mike Bradley battling the House Rock rapids
(Photo by Max Schultz)

Day 2

August the 6th. I knew from the get-go that this was going to be a crucial day – and I knew everybody was looking at this as determining what I would and wouldn't be able to do on the rest of the trip. I didn't sleep much last night. The sound of the rapids kept me awake, as did thinking about whether I should try an intentional roll on one of the "warm-up" rapids we would go through prior to House Rock, as Pete suggested.

I finally made up my mind – and, first thing when I saw Pete this morning, I said, "I'm going to do the roll." I let Chip, Alex and Mike know too. I said, "When I get into the first rapid, I'm going to intentionally flip - you guys call it when we're about halfway through."

They did just that and I flipped myself over when they told me to. More importantly, I rolled right back up without a problem. That eased my mind. I felt like, "Okay, that wasn't too bad, that was all right."

As we approached House Rock, we stopped and some of the group got out and walked ahead to scout it. I stayed and kicked back in my kayak – but before they left, I told them all, "Don't tell me what I'm going to be avoiding, or where things are at, or what's coming – tell me afterwards. If you tell me beforehand to beware of something on my right, I might get turned around and it might end up on my left and I won't know it."

However, with House Rock, there was one big thing Alex *needed* to tell me about - a large hole on the left side of the river that required me to run to the right to avoid it. Alex told me, "I'm going to want you to keep a bow angle at about two o'clock from my voice and keep me on your left - and then once I tell you to punch it, then you're just going to paddle hard and I'll get in front and you'll chase me." I said, "Alright."

But what I was afraid of happening happened. We were lined up perfectly and then, somehow, I don't know what I did, but I crisscrossed and dropped behind him and got him to my right instead of to my left. He told me to make a correction, yelling, "Go right! Go right" – but when I dug my paddle into the water, it got stuck and it flipped me - I rolled right up against the pillow wave on the left and I remember feeling the water coming all up on my side and all along my arm and the side of my head.

The others told me later that "You had about ten to twelve feet of wave above you at that point." It sucked me into it, and I flipped again.

> Alex: *Lonnie ended up going a little further left than I thought he was going to go, and he went into this big powerful "hole" – a bunch of recirculating, exploding water – and I was like "I know he's going to come out of the bottom." So I wasn't super-worried, but I*

thought this would make him hate kayaking, because being in a hole like that is a really scary place to be. It really makes your heart skip a beat, when you're in something like that. So I was like "Man, I hope he's not bummed out about this."

Well, he flipped up on his first try after the hole, and started smiling, yelling and laughing. He was so excited and so stoked. There was no anxiety about what had just happened – instead, he just wanted to know, "Did I do it right? What's going to happen next?" That kind of thing.

That was a very important moment - because I then realized that every one of the rapids that was coming up would be just a problem for us to work through, rather than a place where we would just give up and put Lonnie in the raft. My mindset as a guide totally changed at that point. I committed to getting him through every rapid.

I got through the nastiness of being in that hole and I followed them on over – that's when they just started yelling stuff like, "You did it man!" and "Holy crap! How did you roll in that stuff?"

My answer? "I don't know!"

We were all just screaming, we were all just psyched. Every one of us. It just really set a high tone for the whole river. The big problem was, at this point, Alex and I still don't have the timing and the voice commands down yet. But the more we work together, the better things will get.

Mike: *Wow, we thought, Lonnie made it through House Rock. There were only three or four rapids that were considerably larger coming up on the trip. So now it was no longer a matter of "Can Lonnie do it?", it was more a matter of "Can we do it for Lonnie? Can we make sure that we get him directly where he needs to be and let him go with it?" Lonnie just had great skill. I could not paddle with my eyes blindfolded if I had to. I just rely on my sight. His technique is so perfect! And he can't see. Big, big props to Alex and humongous, humongous props to Mr. Lonnie Bedwell because he's the real deal.*

Alex: *It was an awesome day and the canyon was really, really tight; about 100 yards across at times, and big boils, big whirlpools and stuff like that the whole way down, even in-between the rapids and stuff. It's just amazing to watch Lonnie, someone that can't see, paddle with the water and interact with it so fluidly. It's really amazing to watch.*

Chip: *There was no doubt in my mind that he could do anything in the Grand Canyon so long as he and the guides were communicating well. If we thought there was anything that would compromise his safety on the river, we would opt to walk him around the rapid or do something different. Originally I thought that we might walk like three or four of them, but it was abundantly apparent after House Rock that he was determined and that he was on his game. I think it dawned on all the participants on the trip that Lonnie would be able to navigate them all – even though the bigger rapids were still a big question mark.*

After House Rock, we went through a series of rapids called "The Roaring 20's" – named for the fact that they all fall within the 20 to 30 mile markers on the river. These rapids just get bigger and bigger, and some of them were even more powerful than House Rock. That was good for me, because it had me learning more and more and gave Alex and me more time to work together.

Now, we're camping out again. It's night and it's raining hard. You can hear the water pouring down off the cliff. That brings different worries to me, wondering how much the river's going to rise. Meanwhile, the rain is pounding so hard on everything that once again, I'm not sleeping.

But rain or shine, tomorrow, we'll paddle.

Day 3

August the 7th. Another twelve mile day. We've already done 43 miles on this river.

Today, it was a lot of calm water, nothing difficult. A lot of paddle stroking, a few small rapids – but the last one right before camp kinda got me. I ended up flipping on it, and I rolled twice today. Trying to keep track of how many times I roll down this whole river. Hopefully I can keep getting back up. Also hoping I won't have to swim, because, man, this water's cold.

We stopped at Redwall Cavern, a large alcove, probably 200 yards wide, 100 yards deep. Had a big, sandy floor to it and it was so huge, people could play Frisbee in it. We got back in our boats, floated on down the river, and we stopped at a little-bitty canyon and had dinner. We hiked up to a little place called Nautiloid Canyon, named for the fossils of marine creatures that were something like a cross between a squid and a snail. I felt the fossil imprints in the rocks.

Alex and me in Nautiloid Canyon. (Photo by Mike Bradley)

Just now, somebody with a video camera asked what my thoughts were. I had to say, one thing that hurts is the fact that I can't see any of the canyon. The people describe everything to me – how the Grand Canyon is so vast with so many colors. Then there are the amazing sunsets. It sounds so beautiful, I wish I could see it for myself. For me, it does have its own kind of sound - the birds are a little bit different, for example. The smell is a little different too. I don't really know how to describe it. It's kind of got its own flavor out here.

Alex has been trying to teach me some stroke moves and stuff with my paddle, and how to try maintain balance and do better. It seems like I'm paddling stronger with my right arm than I am with my left, which causes me to shift over in the river to the left-hand side a lot.

We ate like kings tonight. We had steak, mashed potatoes, and it was just absolutely delicious. And salad. Amazing. Just amazing what we're eating.

We've got a wide variety of people with us. I can't believe how all of these gals and guys, all of them have absolutely rallied around me to try to help me do this. They all look out for me, each and every one of them. It's just amazing. The sacrifices made to make this happen is just amazing.

I'm just sitting and thinking of this canyon and how beautiful it must be. No matter what, there's no way in the world that man can create anything that comes close to what God has created. It's something. I'm just - I don't know, just speechless at this experience I'm privileged enough to be a part of.

Day 4

August the 8th. We started out in camp with breakfast and then we headed down a long stretch of little, small stuff. Then we did a hike up to Ancestral Pueblo ground, where some ancient Native American ruins are located.

This was one of those hikes where the other guys didn't have a clue how I was going to manage it. Well, I just kind of put my hand on the shoulder or back of whoever was in front of me and felt along as we climbed up and down the rocks. Today, I was given the nickname of "Lonnie Goat" by Eric Guzman, because he and the rest of them couldn't believe that I was not only kayaking this river, but I was also doing these walks. They're not the easiest hikes in the world, by any means and they thought I'd be just creeping along - but, using whatever hand of mine that was on somebody's back, I would feel the person's motions to tell if they were stepping up or down - and then, with my other hand, I'd use my cane for balance and to find an edge if I knew I'd be exposed on one side. That's how I did it. My thought was, if you guys are going up there, I'm going with you. I'm not staying behind.

Alex guiding me on a canyon hike, followed by Chip Sell.
(photo by Mike Bradley)

Alex: *Lonnie galvanized everybody else in the group. He made the atmosphere of the trip a lot better with his positive attitude. And he went on every single hike with us – he wasn't going to see the amazing views of the Grand Canyon we did, but he would always come with us. For him, he was almost like entertaining us – "I'll go if you want to do that" – but he didn't have any desire to go on those hikes. He'd rather be paddling because that's what he came for, but he'd never complain about that.*

*From left to right: Eric Guzman, Steven Fullers, Mike Bradley, Paul Noeth,
Ashley Crandall, me, Jahzeel Sequeira, Alex and Chip Sell
(Photo by Dale Osborn)*

Then we were back on the river and hit another big rapid. This was one of the first times I really thought I had to work with Alex more and more. If we can hear each other all the way through these rapids coming up, the next three days especially, then we can run this whole canyon. He's incredible. He's absolutely incredible, being able to stick with me, give me commands and letting me know what to do without him having to do it for me.

Chip: *Alex led Lonnie mainly, and then I did a lot of chase-boating along with Mike, shadowing Lonnie from behind. You had to be pretty darn close, especially when he got into the really large rapids, to give directions. Alex would be the lead guide and then it was more a group effort behind Lonnie - half the time I spent back there, half the time Mike was back there, and then some of the other guys jumped in occasionally. The person immediately behind Lonnie would give "left stroke forward," "right stroke forward," "paddle, paddle" – those kinds of commands, trying to keep it simple so if he was going into something, you could say "paddle, paddle, paddle" so he would really reach out and paddle as hard as he could, back paddle if he needed to get away from something, and paddle on the left or right as a correction stroke. If Alex got a little ahead of him or the river was moving him in a direction he shouldn't be going in, we'd throw in a correction stroke.*

Alex: *When I wanted him to go left or right, instead of paddling over to the direction I wanted him to go, I could just yell over that specific shoulder. To him, it would sound like I was five feet to my right, if I were yelling over the right shoulder. That way, I wouldn't have to tell him "Turn right." I could just say "On me." We had to find easy ways to manipulate his position without putting the burden on him, because if I'm in the water and explaining every wave and ripple that's going by, it's just impossible for both of us. That's the battle that a lot of guides that I've worked with have when they are out with blind kayakers. You have to figure out how to keep it as simple as possible when you're helping them navigate. So it took a few days until we were meshing well and paddling well together, and I think a big part of that is just getting to know each other personally too. Before a rapid, some guys get nervous and quiet and don't want to hear too much about it, but Lonnie wasn't like that. He would say, "Tell me what I need to know."*

He was the good kind of nervous. One kind of nervous paralyzes you and makes you do stupid things, and the other focuses you and keeps out any distractions that takes away from your paddling. Usually he operated in that good nervous zone. I think part of what I was doing was getting him to understand when he had to make a move, without him getting too scared about it. To me, the whole thing – guiding Lonnie or anybody else – is

*making sure they're laughing and having fun. If some-
one's scared, they're not having fun.*

Alex and I have gotten the voice commands down to the
point where it works solid, I mean it works really, really solid.
Being able to hear, however, is still sometimes a problem. If
we just had a good solid sound system, like with speakers,
possibly in the kayak behind me, it would make a huge difference. I really did do better today, though. If we can keep to
where I can hear him, I really think we can run this river. I
guess the next few days will really determine that. That part
will be the meat of the river, as far as the water goes. I'm
looking forward to it, I really am looking forward to it.

Again, it's not just Alex, this whole group has got my
back. I know when we leave here, we'll all go our separate
ways again, but it's kind of neat how we're here together
making this happen. For now, I just have to take it one day at
a time, one rapid at a time, and hopefully just run the whole
thing.

Yeah, today was a good day.

Photo by Mike Bradley

Day 5

August the 9th. We did a lot of flat water for the most part. Did a couple of pretty good drops, and we made a stop where the Little Colorado pulls into the Colorado River, around Mile 61. We then hiked up the Little Colorado and hit an area that was muddy, kind of like quicksand. Carmen caked herself with mud and said it was really good for the skin.

Everybody was talking about playing in the mud – so I did. I just did a belly flop and buried my face right into it. They all laughed and started packing mud on top of me. Somebody took a picture of it – and I was so covered in mud, apparently, all you could see was my teeth!

And then I started a mud fight. They were marveling at my aim, saying, "How can you find me?" My answer? "Because you're not shutting up!"

Finally, we got in a side stream to wash off the mud. Then we put our lifejackets on upside down, around our waist like diapers, then we did a train down the Little Colorado back to where our boats were. We just took our legs and wrapped them around the person in front of us, then we all laid on our backs and floated down. Near the bottom, there was a small drop and that's where our diaper/lifejackets came in handy – because when you fell, the lifejacket would cushion the landing.

We're stopped for the night here at around Mile 71, just before a series of some of the bigger rapids on the river. We set up, made camp and had a good spaghetti dinner. Good stuff.

Day 6

August the 10th. We ran from mile marker 71 down to 91 and hit a bunch of major rapids. The first one, Unkar Rapid, was big - and I got me a cold beer coming, even though I don't drink beer that often, because I got through it without flipping.

But then we came up on the Hance Rapid, one of the big, dangerous ones, because there are a lot of huge shards of volcanic rock, which doesn't erode as much as normal rock. Hance Rapid also has the biggest water drop on this run, an average of 30 feet, depending on water level.

The guys went ahead and scouted the Hance, while I laid back in my kayak and got some rest. Alex came back and said, "Are you really that calm? You're calmer than I am, man!"

We talked about the approach. Alex said to me, "We're going to go over river right – we're on river left right now –

and we're going to ferry across the river to the other side, and we're going to drop in river right below this hole, and make a right-to-left move across the river and then run the rest of the river." And then he added, "Whatever you do, Lonnie, don't get squirrelly on me, and don't roll."

So what does Lonnie do? He gets squirrelly and rolls right into the hole.

Alex: *Hance was the rapid I was the most concerned about coming into this trip, and a rapid that I honestly was considering just telling Lonnie to ride it out in the raft. Basically, we started on the right side of the rapid and worked our way through a lot of current going left. To make that move, you have to have a lot of momentum and you get in behind some pretty big holes that are really sticky – but, at the same time, you want to use them, so they can help you get to the left side of the river. As we dropped in, we both caught an edge on this left hole, and since Lonnie can't see, the current swept his boat out from under him and flipped him right into the hole. Before we rode the rapid, I told him "This is a spot you really don't want to roll in" - and that's exactly where he ended up rolling.*

Luckily, he came right up on the other side almost instantly - then the current just pulled him right down where he needed to be. I barely had to do two or three strokes just to slow down so he could catch up to me. He was ready to go and we were perfectly on line in the rapid – it went completely smooth, no worries, really, really fun rapid.

Out of the 5 or 6 kayakers, me, Lonnie and Chip were really the only people that did this leg and won it. That shows how difficult it was to make it over to where you need to be in the rapid.

Hance is one of the longest rapids on the river – probably about a mile long, 45 seconds to get through. You're going fast. That was the first major rapid that we hit, much bigger than anything I've done. Once we did it, such a feeling – like wow, we did it. Alex was like, "Oh gosh man, I can't believe you did that!" I said, "The river was with me man, sometimes you got to get lucky."

That's when Alex told me that Joe Mornini told him NOT to take me through this rapid NO MATTER WHAT. According-ing to Alex, Joe said, "Lonnie will want to run it, but I'm telling you, Alex, don't do it, don't take him through it." I said, "Cool... so why'd you let me do it?" He answered, "I thought we were getting to where we could do it."

Then we came on down and did a bunch of other big rap-ids. One of the last ones, the Horn Creek Rapid, one of the guys said was one of the hardest rapids to run. I was told when I went into it to come in, angle to the left, and paddle hard to the left, and whatever else, don't spin out - because it'll shoot me down the right side which would be completely wrong.

Well, I rolled, flipped upside down, and popped right back up - and when the kayak went upside down, it spit me right back over where I should be and put me on a perfect line to go down the chute. So got very lucky there. But we ran it, and man, there were some big waves. It was pretty cool.

Alex: *We had a couple miles there of pretty continuous, big, big waves – 10, 15 ft. waves. Quarter-mile long rapids - real serious big water, and just beautiful cliffs on either side. Awesome section of the river. It was great because we've worked out the timing, we've worked out the voice commands to the point where, when we got to the biggest rapid of the day, Horn Creek, I felt confident enough to take a little bit more of a challenging approach with Lonnie. The rafts basically moved to the left side of the river for the rapid and then went down a nice smooth tongue, and stayed well away from the right side of the river. The reason for that is because the right side had some of the biggest reactionary waves I've ever seen; I've kayaked a lot of rivers and lots of high water, and I've never seen waves that are as big or as powerful as the waves that were on the right side of the river. That being said, they were very clean; there weren't any rocks sticking out of them or anything like that. They were just really, really big rapids.*

Taking on the Horn Creek rapid.

Because I felt confident with the commands and the timing that we worked out over the last six days, we started on the right side and we went across one of the biggest lateral waves I think there is on a river. A lateral wave is one that breaks towards the center of the river and can throw you completely off. I hit that huge lateral and just tucked in tight to the boat – and I felt another wave curl over my head from the right side, it just engulfed me. I just stayed curled up and came up outside the back side of the wave, and looked over my left shoulder...and Lonnie was launching over a wave. He's got a perfect position on top of the wave, a real strong forward stroke, and he just moved perfectly over the wave. It was one of the coolest things I've seen that a kayaker do on the river. It was beautiful, beautiful kayaking.

As soon as we made it past that lateral, we entered into the wave train, which was filled with huge spiking, reactionary waves coming from all sides. We just kept our paddles pointed downstream and we got flushed down through the big waves – waves of that size and rapids that strong have the tendency to make you feel really, really small. That's definitely how I felt paddling today – I just felt tiny on this huge body of water. Just so deep. I'm used to running rapids where you see the rocks under the water a lot of times. Here, the rocks might be thirty or forty feet under you, but they're big enough and there's enough water that they cause these huge waves to form. It makes you feel powerless, but it's really cool to be a part of something so big and strong, and to be able to move so successfully through it.

It's really fun paddling with Lonnie at this point, because I know that wherever I go and whatever approach I want to make, we can get it and it won't be an issue because we have the timing worked out. His fundamentals are so solid; it's amazing to see him paddle without any sort of apprehension or fear about the waves that are coming - he just focuses on the fundamentals and that's what helps him paddle so well.

A lot of people that I've taught to kayak over the years get caught up in what's going on around them – in these big waves, in this powerful place, and they feel scared and out of control. They end up putting themselves in a bad place because they're not sticking to the fundamental skills. Lonnie doesn't have to worry about any of that – he focuses on where he's at, and how the water feels under his boat and on his paddle, and it's amazing how successful and how graceful it is when you kayak with that mentality. When I see him kayak, I see that – it's perfectly invisible. It's really fun to watch.

Definitely felt a sense of accomplishment today; glad we didn't have any issues and now that those big rapids are out of the way – the ones I was seriously considering having Lonnie sit in the raft for – we have a lot of confidence and momentum going into the second half of the trip. There are still really serious rapids and tight gorges, but we kind of hit the crux today and the rest is going to be sticking with what we know works and enjoying the place we're at.

One of our group, Ashley, is a wounded vet who's disabled. It's her first time out here paddling a support raft. She came out here in a kayak before, but they asked her to be on the raft this time. She had never paddled one before in her life, and she ran this whole thing clean to this point. It's just amazing. It's all just worked out, and the group – they're all just a bunch of good people having a good time.

Hopefully I'll get a good night's sleep - last night, I didn't sleep but two or three hours. Man, I don't know, it's just an extraordinary experience and over a hundred miles still to go. I just hope things keep going well for all of us. What a day, what a day.

The rapids today were some of the toughest on the river. There's a whole line of them again tomorrow, but today we made it through two of the biggest ones. We just did it. It was the first time I thought, "Man, I can make this without doing any swims." And Alex agreed – he thought I could do it too without swimming. Just rolling when I flip and getting back on track.

It could be done.

> *Alex: We got to a point where it was one of the last few days of the really hard rapids, and Lonnie hadn't swum yet. And many others on the trip had. There was this question hanging in the air - "Is he going to do this whole river without swimming?" For me, as a guide, that would have been the coolest thing ever.*
>
> *So our focus shifted from just enjoying the river and the rapids to reaching this incredible goal – a goal that we created on the fly.*

Day 7

August the 11th, our second day of big rapids.

We started out at Granite Rapid, which is one of the most turbulent rapids in the whole river - there's no real pattern to it, you get laterals from all directions so you get hit from all directions. And it gave Alex and me quite a moment – him much more so than me, because I had no idea the kind of danger I was in. Sometimes, being blind has its advantages!

> *Alex: Granite had a couple of really big holes on the right side, and a piece of the wall that stuck out on the left. I decided to take Lonnie and me through the center of the rapid and then a little bit to the left – to avoid the holes. I figured as soon as we got past the second hole, we would make a hard right and then a hard left to get around a rock island in the middle of the river.*
>
> *It got exciting. We made it around the holes just fine, we dropped in just fine and then a wave came and*

turned Lonnie's bow to the left. Since we were already left-center to the rapid, we were already really close to the wall at that point. I got a little bit nervous and wanted to tell him to turn right, but in order to have him hear me over the waves, I had to turn my boat around.

When I made that maneuver, I said "Hard right!" – and then a wave immediately got on top of me and flipped me instantly. That was my first flip on the river - I was underwater and I felt terrible because I couldn't guide Lonnie and I knew he was in a really bad spot. He was in a place where I knew I wouldn't want to be in a kayak, getting pushed into that left wall.

I tried to roll back up as fast as I could, and as soon as I did, I saw he was still heading left towards the wall – and he was still paddling hard because I guess he thought I was in front of him still. I just yelled as loud as I could, "Turn right, turn right!" – but I couldn't yell loud enough. He wasn't hearing me.

Finally, he made out what I was saying and made a real hard right turn - and as soon as he did, a big lateral hit him from the right side and flipped him instantly. At that point, I was pretty freaked out – definitely as nervous as I've been on this trip so far – because I really didn't want him to get pushed into that wall.

He couldn't get a good roll right off the bat – he got a little bit of air, and then went back under. And when that happened, Lonnie was probably 10 to 15 feet away from the wall on the left wall - and we were moving 15 to 20 miles an hour. I definitely didn't want him to hit the rock wall going at that speed, going that fast.

When I was upside down and underwater for that long, I felt the fury of the water and I was like, "Man!" It was going through my mind, "You don't want to swim this, you don't want to swim this. It will be ugly. Just stick it out, just stick it out, just stick it out." But I couldn't get my paddle to the surface, I couldn't roll up, I just remember sitting upside down in the water, thinking, "Man, this is cold, this is brutal."

And I was running out of air.

I knew I couldn't do a roll, but I had to try to breathe - so I pulled up as hard as I could to roll and I literally felt the waterline at my chin. I got a gasp of air, back under I went, and I was upside down again. That's when I really realized the power of that river, it was like being upside down in a washing machine whose agitation mode was on steroids.

I set up to try to roll again, because the water had calmed down enough for me to find the surface. Just started to do my rolling and then it flipped right up, and I was like, "What happened?" What happened was Alex – who reached out and grabbed me and helped me complete the roll. You just realize the power and the fury of this whole river when you're doing that stuff.

Mike: *That's the other thing that Joe had told me. If he flips, just remember, he's okay. When you think he can't hold his breath any longer, he'll still hold his breath. And Joe was right. Lonnie would sometimes pop right back up and other times, we would all be watching the bottom of his boat float down the river, float down the rapids, waiting for him to do the roll, and all of a sudden Lonnie would pop back up, appearing to be as calm as can be. He doesn't let that anxiety and fear of the unknown affect him.*

Alex: *Luckily, while Lonnie was upside down and heading for the rock wall, we hit a really big lateral that shoved us right back into the current of the river and out of danger. I remember just getting hit by that big wall of water and just being so happy - because it got us away from that wall and gave me the little bit of time I needed to catch up to him. I was able to flip him back over and get him squared away in the right direction again, and we paddled through the rest of it without any problems at all.*

It was definitely a little nerve-wracking for me – but not for him, because he couldn't see that wall closing in as fast as it was! It was a blessing that we hit that left lateral when we did and it was definitely a blessing to paddle away from that wall unscathed. It's weird how it works sometimes, and this has happened to me a lot on the river, where a rapid is serious but you still underestimate its power because you're overconfident. And then when you get pushed into a bad place like we were, it just takes a fraction of a second to compromise all that confidence you built on the river.

It was a wake-up call for me, and definitely exhausting. I actually lost my voice because I kept yelling "Go right, go right, go right" as loud as I could. But Lonnie had a ton of composure the whole time. He knew I was a little panicked there – I didn't want him to get pushed into that wall, and he heard it in my voice.

After the rapid, we all kind of had that shaky, adrenaline-filled moment where everyone's happy that we made it down, and happy that it's over and at the same time, just kind of scared. And that's good – a river this size with this much water flowing through in this much of a wilderness setting, it should scare you. It reminded me how fortunate we are to make it down this river this far and to have this tremendous opportunity.

We took lunch right after that; it was a good break for me. I needed a little bit of time to get my wits about me and get some food in me.

We dropped into the "Gems" right after lunch – which is one of my favorite sections of the canyon. It's basically four or five rapids, Agate, Sapphire, Turquoise, Emerald and Ruby, a half mile to three-quarters of a mile apart, and each one's about a quarter mile long - and they're each made up of twisty wave trains. We did really good; we found our lines, we did good angling, we had really good timing and we worked our way down perfectly.

We ended on a rapid called Serpentine, which is the last big one in this section of river, and I've got to tell you – I paddled most of it backwards so I could just enjoy watching Lonnie do his thing, and it was beautiful. Big, big strokes, huge waves, and his boat was a good 3 to 4 feet out of the water coming out of those big waves. It's really cool when I paddle backwards on these big wave trains because I get to see Lonnie doing all these strokes and making all these moves that all kayakers would like to make – just meshing with the river and feeling the rhythm of the river. We all want to get to that same rhythm but he's there.

When I look past him and I see the other kayakers in the group and they're, a lot of times, just getting worked – paddling 10 times harder than they need to, getting flipped, making two or three tries to get up on a roll and that kind of thing. But Lonnie is just powering through these rapids, catching air on the top and squaring each one and just looking like a pro. It's really, really fun to be a part of that. All I'm doing is telling him where I'm at and trying to get his bow pointed in the right direction. Some people paddle for five, six, seven years and they'll never be at that level that he's at right now - and these are people that can see! It's very evident that Lonnie is as much a part of this river as any other kayaker that I've been able to paddle with. It's been awesome to watch it happen.

After we did our last rapid today, there was a pool and you could kind of see the canyon fading away behind us as we came into the rapid, and a big valley opening up in front of us. It was a really big feeling, this really big experience where this world that we've been living that's a half of a mile wide and a couple thousand feet high just kind of gave way to this huge, huge valley. Just felt like, "Hey, we made it through this section and that's good."

I know we've got a lot more miles to get under our belt. But I'd also be willing to bet my first three years of pay - after I get a job - that Lonnie's not going to be stopped and he's going to have a great time on the rest of the trip.

I can remember coming through the Gems and hearing Chip laughing behind me – for no reason, as far as I could tell. So I turned and asked him, "What have you been laughing about?" He said, "Just watching you and Alex is so cool. It's like watching you two dance. I can't believe what I'm seeing." He said it was such a joy watching us do that – it just made me happy.

As I was coming into camp tonight, I thought about the fact that we had actually gotten through the "meat" of the river. Granite was the second of three rapids that Joe had said I probably wouldn't be able to do – but I had done it, despite spending a little too much time underwater and upside down. That meant there was only one more rapid that would be a real challenge – Lava Falls, described as the scariest ten seconds you can have on the Colorado River. But that would be near the end of the trip.

Somebody said to me tonight, "You know, when they told me that you were coming on, I said, 'Oh, so we got a token blind person here.' But that's not at all the case. You're doing awesome." I took that as a very, very good compliment. And Pete, he made a comment, "Absolutely impressive."

Marc Huster, who mainly worked one of the support rafts, had some whiskey, Breckenridge was the name of it - Breckenridge Colorado Bourbon Whiskey. He asked me if I wanted a taste of it, and I took it. Then I asked him if he'd have a shot with me, and he said, "It'd be an absolute privilege." He toasted me with it, and it was a good time. Those kind of things make you feel pretty good.

This was a real, real, real good day.

Photo by Dale Osborn

Day 8

August the 12th. Started out - not so great. I got hardly any sleep last night, maybe an hour.

Sleep has been a big problem on this trip. The rest of the group likes to camp just above the rapids - to them, it's soothing and they love to hear the sounds of the river. To me? It's like being in a torture chamber. I wanted to camp away from the rapids, because when I lay my head down at night, I can't hear the birds or any other sounds of the night that might be more soothing – only the rush of the rapids, all night long. If I had known it was going to be like this, I would have brought one of the books on tape I like to listen to – that would have helped me refocus my mind and forget about the water. But I didn't and I'm stuck. Alex and Mike try their best to tuck me in a ledge or somewhere to cut the noise, but still, that doesn't always work for me.

And last night was the worst – no sleep. It was just grueling. And getting up this morning wasn't any better. We ran a rattlesnake out of camp and Alex shook a scorpion out of my wet suit.

Alex: *Lonnie wakes up and says "I didn't sleep last night." He's upset and cranky. He tells me his boat doesn't feel right – for me, that doesn't mean anything because I don't know what that means. I thought he was just tired.*

So we start paddling out and we get into some really big rapids. I was shocked. Stuff that was totally manageable a day or two ago, Lonnie was suddenly struggling with. I felt scared, because I knew we had bigger rapids coming up.

It was like I had absolutely no control of my kayak whatsoever. Couldn't get my thigh braces to work, couldn't get hardly anything to work. Did some rolls, and actually, Chip bailed me out twice today on two different rapids – once he did what's called a bow rescue and helped me roll back up by jamming his kayak into mine, and the other time, he just reached in and pulled me back up.

Then I figured out the problem, after my one leg popped out of the thigh brace inside the kayak when I tried to do a roll. I felt down along the brace and I could tell that some of its screws were actually coming loose. I relied on the thigh braces to keep my legs tightly connected to the kayak – if one of those braces wasn't connected correctly, that would have a major effect on my control of the boat. That explained why the boat hadn't felt right all day - but I couldn't stop and fix it because we still had more rapids to go. I had to tough it out.

It's an uneasy feeling. All that confidence that I had built over the past week just got shot. Just went straight out the window. So now I'm sitting here, trying to figure it out - hoping it was the thigh brace, instead of me being pathetic.

Alex: *He seemed really frustrated. We kept going down the river and he ends up going into a pretty big rapid upside down and wasn't able to roll up all the way. I was concerned – something was going on that I didn't understand.*

When he came out of his boat for lunch, we looked at the kayak and saw the whole thigh brace had actually come undone. That's a game-changer for someone who can't see and whose only connection to the water is that boat. I was disappointed in myself – when he said his boat didn't feel right, I should have pulled over.

We fixed his boat and ended up having a really good day.

I did end up rolling again, because I couldn't keep my balance. For me, not being able to lock my knee in real tight affected my ability to separate my upper body from my lower body and made me feel like I was teeter-tottering with the river flowing underneath me.

With all the trouble I was having, Chip, Mike and Alex really worked extra, extra hard to stay around me, so, if I did roll, which I did a couple times, they could help get me up. It was definitely a tough, frustrating morning. When we were able to stop, I told everybody I had to lay down and take a little nap. I threw a pad on the ground and laid on it. Then suddenly I got bit by them red ants, once on my right chin and once on my right shoulder. Those suckers sting and burn for, I don't know, about 12 hours or so. So basically, in the span of 24 hours, I had gotten the worst the canyon wildlife had to offer.

On the other hand, we got to hike to a little waterfall and people took turns jumping into the pool at the bottom of it. We had a lot of fun doing that. When we do all of these walks up and down through these places, Mike Plourde, the other Mike on the trip (since Bradley said he was the "good-looking Mike," we called Plourde "Um" for Ugly Mike) always makes it a point to walk behind me and always checks on how I'm doing. If I look a little unsteady, he'll touch my forearm or shoulder, whatever. He's absolutely taking it upon himself to make sure I don't slip and fall and get hurt on any of this stuff.

It's awful neat how everyone's pulling in for me and helping me. Man, I can't say what it means to me. What a group of people can do when they're all focused and working together on the same page is just absolutely amazing. I hope I don't forget to take my time to thank everybody when we're doing this. It makes you realize something about all of us here on Earth - why we can't get together all the time and just enjoy life and not struggle and fight over power, control and whatever else we seem to want to argue over? Why can't we come together like this and enjoy life everywhere?

Mike Bradley, me and, directly behind me, Mike Plourde. (Photo by Dale Osborn)

Afternoon on the river turned out better when they fixed my right thigh brace. Felt a lot better back in the boat again. We stopped at Mile 120 out of 226, so we're over halfway done - Day 8 of 16.

Day 9

Day 9, August the 13th.

We got up a little bit late and walked up to Blacktail Canyon, a really neat little canyon where it's just so utterly quiet. The legends say it's where the Native Americans believed the spirits of the dead ascended. You can literally hear a pin drop in there.

After we did that, we came back down and had breakfast down on the river. Then we ran three major rapids – the Spectre, Bedrock and Deubendorf rapids. We didn't even stop for lunch, we just ran straight through. But I wasn't hungry because we had such a late breakfast. Feeling a whole lot better than the day before. Got stuck once in Bedrock, when my paddle got hung up below on something. I couldn't get it out and ended up rolling. Deubendorf was just an absolute blast. We went in it clean, big waves, just fun. Did really well on that, and kind of got a little bit of confidence back again.

Day 10

August the 14th.

We got up early and we left camp. We had breakfast and took a little three mile jaunt down to a place called Deer Creek Falls, where there was a great big waterfall. We hiked up some of the canyon to the top of the falls, a place they call the Patio.

The canyon gets narrow, but there are places where it gets 10 feet wide. One of the things the Native Americans would do here, in order to prove their manhood, was attempt to jump across the gorge. If they didn't make it, it was a 200 foot drop into the canyon. If they made it, then they would take this white, chalky stuff, cover their hands with it, and use it to leave their handprints on the walls. I was told you can still see some of those handprints on the walls today.

Alex: *Deer Creek is really amazing. We had to take a really sketchy scramble up the canyon wall, about 200 to 300 feet. Once we got up to that level, we dipped into a really tight box canyon with vertical walls that go several hundred feet up and down, and we kind of skirted along the edge of that canyon. It was pretty scary for me, leading Lonnie up there, but, at this point in the trip I know that he has no problem getting up to those places. Luckily, there was no wind - his balance was perfect and he did great.*

We then sat up in an area called the Patio, which is an area where, right before the water plunges into the deep part of the box canyon, it flattens out. Everyone laid out in the shade of some cottonwood trees, and just relaxed. It was a beautiful place – an oasis in the desert. After seeing nothing but rocks and soaring cliffs for the last week or so, it's nice to be around some trees again. Little breeze going through there – good temperature.

From there, I went up to the Room of Thrones, which as far as my experience in the Grand Canyon goes is one of the most magical places. It's another several hundred feet up in elevation from the Patio - you follow this stream up into this wide valley up above the first level of cliffs above the canyon. It's the most brutally hot, arid, and desolate region I've hiked through in my life; it's just crazy in there. You come out into that valley and then you kind of dip back down towards the stream, and then across the stream and then you go up on the other side of the valley. Again it's just brutally hot, there's no shade, and as you climb higher, it becomes more of a boulder garden. You do more scrambling and you keep climbing and climbing, and finally you reach this part of the cliff that's been carved out – so it's overhanging – and there's a waterfall that drops right on the side of it. The water that forms Deer Creek actually comes out of the side of the cliff, and it falls about 100 feet or so from that crack in the wall – just falls straight out of the rock. It's amazing. That stream falling out is ice cold and it makes this really cool draft from the cold air around the water.

In that little alcove, people have gone in there and set up boulders and stones to look like "thrones" – that's why it's called the Room of Thrones, and there's about 20 of these chairs that have just been made out of the shale that's fallen out of the cliffs over the years.

We then floated on down the river just about a mile, and pulled in for the night. Couple of guides from another group, just up over the sand here a little bit, walked over and brought us some more ice and everyone sat down, had a few drinks and shot the breeze.

Day 11

August 15th. Got up and got started. After breakfast, did about 11 miles down the river. Few little rapids. Only rolled once today, and that was okay. Only on the water for about 2 ½ hours.

We set up camp, then I took a little nap. When I got up, the wind was blowing bad. I was actually in the tent, but the wind was coming at it so hard that it literally blew sand right through the sides. Then it got worse – the wind picked the tent up with me in it and flipped me over a couple of times. I was like, "Holy Crap!" I was wondering if it was going to stop before the tent and me got blown right into the river. We had to put some small boulders on each corner of the tent to keep it in place.

The rest of the day was pretty chill. I decided to trim some of my beard off to make it a Fu Manchu. Something to do. One of the cook crew cooked barbeque pork chops for dinner. Man, they were outstanding. Then they cooked steak, chicken and barbeque pork chops.

A lot of people are starting to get homesick and getting ready to get back to family. Problem here is there's no contact here unless you have a satellite phone to call out of here, and only one of us has one.

It was a good day. Good day on the river, good day sitting here in camp.

Alex: *We had already run most of all the rapids that are named and well-known in the Grand Canyon, and Day 10 and 11 were a couple of real short days. Yesterday we moved about 10 miles, but we did it all before lunch, so we were able to set up camp and lunch at the same time. The day before that, we only moved downriver 3 or 4 miles, and, again, we set up lunch and camp at the same time.*

Yesterday I took a nap for the first time on the trip, and I just felt a little groggy throughout the afternoon; I think that's a combination of the sun, the exposure, a little bit of the wind, and obviously the heat. It's a hard place to live, and I think the group of paddlers – the 16 people here – are kind of feeling it. We're doing shorter days and trying to enjoy the sight hikes as much as we can.

Day 12

August the 16th. We got up out of camp early, had to run a rapid called Upset and that's exactly what it did to me! The place was full of laterals, like Granite, and I knew I was going to have an issue with them. Sure enough, one came in from the left, and I hit it. Then there was a second one and a third one. The second one just rolled me. I tried to roll up right away, but then the third one hit and took me right back under. And this time, when I tried to roll back up, disaster struck.

My kayak skirt imploded.

> Mike: *A kayak skirt is made of neoprene (a rubber synthetic) and attaches around your waist as you sit in the kayak - it keeps your boat from taking on water, which happens all too easily when you're going through whitewater. But when it implodes, the force of the water pushes the skirt down and makes it almost impossible to roll back up - because the boat is now all full of water. So yeah, when that happened to Lonnie, he lost his kayak.*

There I was upside down in a kayak full of water. What else could I do? I knew all my guides were close to where I was, so I just slid out from under my kayak into the river, came to the surface and quickly found (and grabbed) the back of Chip's kayak. Meanwhile, the others got hold of my kayak, so it wouldn't keep traveling down the river on its own. Then, we all went over to the side of the river bank, where I got back into my kayak and went back out. It had all happened so fast that we were all back on the river before the support rafts had reached us.

So that was it. I had had to do a small swim – my first swim on the trip. One of my major goals had fallen, which really made me angry. But, I have to say, looking back on it all, I had made it that far without losing my boat. And luckily, I wasn't hurt – only my boat had gotten injured, as it now had a few cracks on top.

Still, Upset upset me tremendously. I have to admit, before I got here, from everything Joe told me, I was positive I would be swimming a lot. But once I got through Day 7, I thought I might make it all the way without that happening. The only rapid I was at all anxious about at this point was Lava Falls - the Upset rapid wasn't even a concern. So how did I end up swimming *there*?

You never know, man.

Mikes Bradley and Plourde scout the rapids with Alex. (Photo provided by Mike Bradley)

Day 13

August 17th. Lava Falls. Our last main challenge.

We got up and ran a lot of easy flat water. Before we reached Lava Falls, the guys stopped and went ahead and scouted it. I was worried - a storm had been following us most of the way down the river but hadn't quite caught us. I was hoping the scouting expedition would be a quick one...but no, they took their time and had a few snacks along the way. I'm like, "Guys, hurry and do a quick scout so we can beat this storm." Well, they didn't make it quick, I sat there waiting and we all ended up paying the price.

> Alex: *We were sitting on the side of the river and he could sense the storm coming – he kept saying, "Let's go!" because he didn't want the wind to catch the rapid – so it ended up hitting us right before we went into Lava Falls.*

By the time we got back in the boats, the storm caught us.

The wind just came at us in a big way and really hit the support rafts hard. Kelly (better known to us as "Boy Howdy"), who ran the lead raft the whole trip, got turned right around – she ended up running the whole rapid backwards, but she was okay. Ashley, who was driving the support raft that had my gear in it, got blown sideways, almost going upside down twice, but she managed to stay afloat. One of the straps holding a gear bag snapped and went into the water. Nobody knows how Ashley managed to stay on the raft, but she did, without getting flipped or having to go swimming. Max got knocked off his raft briefly.

Alex thought we had a good plan to handle Lava Falls, but the wind took care of that.

Lava Falls. One of those guys is me. (Photo by Dale Osborn)

Alex: *We got hit by this huge gust of wind. It was scary for both of us. I went through a really big breaking wave and I turned around to see where he was...and I just saw his boat just shoot up into the air. His kayak just exploded out of the water, like a dolphin jumping out of the water! And he made a very dramatic exit from his boat.*

I flipped and dang if my skirt didn't implode again! I was upside down in the water, wondering if there was any way to roll, when the water just slammed me and ripped me out of my kayak! I was pulled down under the water and the kayak went flying up in the air.

Using both hands, I was hanging on for dear life to my paddle – I was extended straight forward, holding the paddle out in front of me and getting spun around like I was holding a rotating helicopter blade. Then I finally managed to pull in the paddle – and then the water started spinning me head-over-heels, so I was doing somersaults.

Alex: *I saw him, in the eddy right below. Of course, he can't see, so when he swims, it's really dangerous. And he gets sucked into this eddy that's right before this really big wave, and the eddy had a current pulling the water and Lonnie towards that big wave – bad place to go, but he can't tell because he can't see. I'm like, "I've got to get him."*

I finally popped up out of the water and got some air. I hear Alex go, "Amazing!" But I wasn't impressed. I was just mad. In my mind, my friggin' skirt had imploded again and I didn't get the chance to run one of the biggest rapids because of it. I started yelling about it so forcefully, that I scared Alex away! I just heard him paddling away from me.

Alex: *I'm paddling toward him, calling his name, and then he comes up out of the water. I get up close to him and I see he's livid – absolutely livid. Here I'm thinking he would be terrified and freaked out – but no, not Lonnie. He's punching the water and yelling, saying "I can't believe I swam! I didn't get a chance!" I was afraid to let him grab my boat to hang on, because he was so mad, I thought he might hit me! I was shocked at how angry he was. Not at me, luckily. Later, we had a good laugh out of that. I ended up pulling him out, and we celebrated making it through Lava Falls alive, which is a Grand Canyon tradition.*

The frustrating thing was that it wasn't about my kayaking ability, it was about the bad equipment. Alex said that he really truly believed that if I had had a good skirt and a better kayak, I wouldn't have had to swim.

Alex: *If it hadn't been for the minor equipment defects in regard to the boat and the skirt, I truly believe he would have never swam this entire run. He ended up in the water at both Upset and Lava Falls because his skirt imploded, no fault of Lonnie's. It was just an equipment problem, you can't control that stuff. None of the gear he was using here is gear he had at home, and he made it work. That's the thing about Lonnie on this whole trip, he made it work. He can't see the waves, he can't see all the laterals, I do my best to line it up and put him in the right spot – but what it comes down to is that he makes it all work. He takes what he feels and what he hears from me and he does more with that small amount of information than a lot of other paddlers would. And it's amazing.*

So that was my trip down Lava. It wasn't my best and I would have loved to try it 15 minutes earlier, before we had to fight the windstorm along with the rapids. But that didn't happen - and it might have been the same outcome anyway - who knows.

That was the last of the hard rapids on the river. We're now about a mile down from Lava, where we're going to spend the night.

Day 14

August the 18th. Wind and rain picked up last night and, man, that made for a noisy night. Today, I'm running on about 30 minutes to an hour of sleep. I'm thinking I made it this far with only two swims, I sure wasn't thinking that going in. I'm still pretty pleased with the run we've got so far and definitely with this great group of people.

Today, we took off from Mile 181 and made it to 199. This stretch was a lot of calm water. No big rapids; just more little ripples than anything. A few smaller, little wave trains and a lot of swirly water. The canyon at this point kind of opened up really, really wide – felt very different than what we've been going through.

Photo by Dale Osborn

We got in probably about 2 pm this afternoon to set up camp - and then got hit with a heck of a rainstorm. Big wind, thunder and lightning, and then it blew through after a little bit. I laid down, slept about three hours in the middle of the afternoon, and then got up and washed my clothes in the river. Had some dinner.

Sitting here, thinking about tomorrow - three supposedly pretty significant rapids, and that will be the end of the bigger rapids on this trip. Tomorrow night will be our last night on the river.

I kind of think of this river as like life. We get bored with the quiet peaceful parts, then we get caught up in the utter chaos of the rapids, something that's so big and so powerful. You feel so out of control that you think, "I'm done with this. I want to get back to the calm." If you can't find your way through that chaos, then you're looking for the calm again. If you do find a way through that chaos, then it doesn't bother you so much. As a matter of fact, you want *more* of that chaos. That's human nature.

Definitely interesting and a rewarding trip. We'll see what tomorrow brings.

Day 15

August 19th. Today didn't turn out to be quite as uneventful as I thought.

205 Mile Rapid is named for the mile marker it's located at. And I will remember that actual physical mile marker for the rest of my life. I hit the wave train head on, but then it broke over the top of me just as I was going up on top of it – and it literally back-flipped me in the kayak!

> Mike: *He came up off of a wave just as it was peaking, and he came up off the crest of that wave and I...well, I saw Lonnie upside down. Lonnie had done a backflip off the top of this wave and broke his glasses...*

...on the mile marker. It hit me in the face so hard it snapped my dark glasses in half and back-flipped me in the kayak. I landed in the water and flipped upside down in my boat, then I rolled back up and kept paddling. And I started laughing my butt off. Mike looked at me and said, "What the hell are you laughing at?" I said, "I never been back-flipped in a kayak before!" Then he laughed too and said, "Man, only you can take a beat down like that and come up laughing!"

Next on the agenda, right after the 205 Rapid, was the 209 Mile Rapid. I guess at this point, whoever scouted this river got too tired to think of any more names. Anyway, I was about to be very glad that Mike was kayaking right behind me.

The 209 Rapid's big danger was in the center – where it dropped into a big hole. I went over to the left like I was supposed to, when a whirlpool suddenly just spun me right around and flipped me. I rolled right back up, but when I did, I was now headed the exact wrong way. I caught the edge of the hole and ended up circling its rim.

> Mike: *That was one time that I was scared for Lonnie. We had to stay river left to avoid a massive hole that took up the entire channel of the river. So I was behind Lonnie when the whirlpool spun his boat out of the main current. He was being sucked into this massive hole and I was looking at him going, "Oh no, oh no."*
>
> *I had to make a split second decision on what I was going to do. I figured it was better for me to be in the hole then for Lonnie, because I would be able to deal with it better. I would be able to see what I was moving into and could better react. But then I thought again - maybe if I got enough power going, I could get both of us out.*
>
> *So I built up as much speed and momentum as I could in my kayak and slammed my boat into Lonnie's – and as I'm slamming into him, I'm yelling, "It's me, It's me, I've got you, keep paddling!" I wanted him to know what was going on. Fortunately, neither one of us ended up in the hole.*

Tonight is our last on the river. We sat around, just talking, telling stories. I told the whole group about when my family asked me why I was going to do this trip when it seemed so crazy – and I told them that every paddle stroke I make is an effort to pay back all the men and women who served overseas for the sacrifices they've made on my behalf. I can't make enough paddle strokes to fully repay that debt, but I will do what I can to get as close as possible.

My turn on the cooking crew.

I also told the group that it was only fitting that I swam. Even if I would have run the river clean, my first try wouldn't have been good enough and the river was just letting me know that.

Day 16

August the 20th. Last day on the river.

Only one slightly close call from a lateral but no big deal. We stopped just after the last rapid, about halfway to where we would be leaving the river and ending our journey. Everybody was feeling emotional about what we had done.

Chip: *At that point, they went and grabbed the American flag off one of the support rafts and stuck it behind Lonnie's lifejacket. Everyone seemed calm, but it was anything but calm - everyone felt like, "Oh my God, Lonnie just did it. The whole Grand Canyon!" Absolutely amazing to be a part of that.*

Alex: *Another tradition about this trip: during the last few miles, you don't say a word – no one in the group says a word for a few hours. Still, Lonnie can't see where he's going so I still have to quietly guide him here and there. But for the most part, we just paddled on, lost in our thoughts.*

Mike: *So Lonnie was paddling with this flag hoisted above him from the back of his lifejacket. As I was watching him paddle, I could just see in his face that he wanted to let it out, he wanted to scream, with some kind of "I know I did it" howl of success. But he also knew the tradition that he wasn't supposed to make any sound.*

I paddled over by his side and finally said, "It's okay - you can let it out." And Lonnie just let loose with this yell of excitement - and the look on his face as he was shouting was incredible. The thing about Lonnie was that he never once said "I did this, I was successful." He always said, "We were successful." To Lonnie, it was always "we."

Alex: *Lonnie just let out this warrior cry. Just yells at the top of his lungs and hits the water, he was just so happy and excited to be where we were with the people we were with. It represented the way all of us were feeling. A lot of people on and before the trip had a lot of apprehension about Lonnie trying this. That yell, to me, was like, "Yes, we can do that."*

For me, it was a big deal because after the trip, I was going to go home, go back with my friends and have to explain why I led a blind kayaker down this dangerous water. A lot of the time, I didn't really know if this was a responsible thing for me to do with Lonnie. It was going through my head for most of the trip – "Is this the safest idea?"

But Joe Mornini actually played a big role in why I wanted Lonnie to paddle all those big rapids. He told me "If you have any doubts, put Lonnie in the raft," that was officially what he had to tell me. But I knew the unofficial side of Joe was saying, "Go, do it, see if it's possible." That's the kind of guy that Joe is.

End of the journey. With Jahzeel Sequeira, Alex and Mike.
(Photo by Dale Osborn)

It took a while for us to get off the river – there had been a big flash flood the night before and it had completely washed out the road going into the canyon. We weren't even sure we would be able to get out that day, but they brought in bulldozers to clear it out.

The next day, as we were getting ready to fly back home, I was surprised to find out that nobody had called Joe to tell him what happened on the trip! This was the guy that made this whole thing possible – and was anxious to find out how I had done.

> Joe: *While Lonnie was in the canyon, I was very stressed. There was no news about what was going on. I was the guy who had authorized a blind veteran to run some of the biggest whitewater in the country. I was very anxious about the whole thing and needed to know that everyone was out safety.*
>
> *Lonnie finally called me when I was driving the Team River Runner van and trailer to a wounded warrior paddling session. I can remember the exact place I was when I answered my phone. Lonnie was on the other end saying, "Hey Joe, It's Lonnie!" and I'm like, "Hey Lonnie, you're okay?" "I'm fine." "Everyone else okay?" "No one's hurt, we're all good" and then I let out with a big "Whooo!"*
>
> *But then Lonnie says, "Joe, I got to tell you. I didn't make it. I didn't run the whole thing." Well, I pretty much expected he wouldn't, and I said, "Hey, that's okay, man, that's okay, I'm good with that. You went in there and made a real effort..."*
>
> *That's when Lonnie said, "Joe, I'm kidding. I ran the whole thing."*

When I told him I ran the whole thing and I only swam a couple of times, didn't go in the raft or walk around any of the rapids, Joe started crying. He said, "Do you realize what you've just done?" And he had to pull over. And he said, "I got to stop." And that made me feel just how much this meant to him. He was so overcome that we couldn't talk long. We agreed to talk it through the next day instead.

I got kind of emotional at that time, I had to pull over, so I could get my shit together before I headed onto the river. I was pretty much overwhelmed. It was a huge thing for Lonnie. The first thing I thought was, "Here's this guy who's blind and he achieved this. He must feel like he's a thousand feet tall - even though he couldn't see what he did, he must have felt it. The second thing I thought was, "Wow, this is going mean a lot to people who have disabilities. They'll say, "Are you kidding me? I want to do that too."

And sure enough, wounded and blind vets from across the country became inspired by Lonnie's example. He did this to help others. He's a noble person who sees clearer than people who have 20/20 vision. He's become a huge ambassador in the Team River Runner system.

Mike: *It was amazing to be a part of that. There's nothing that compares to the feeling that I had on the river. It was an incredible experience and definitely created some lifelong friendships. I also experienced things I needed to experience. Lonnie is an amazing person, very genuine. To be able to associate with an individual like that is an honor to me.*

Alex: *Lonnie and I bonded on the water, and for me at this point in my life, Lonnie's a little bit like a father figure. He's had experiences and gone through things I can't even imagine. He has such a positive attitude about things – and he taught me how to live my life a little bit better and be a better person. I was very emotional when the whole trip was over. We went through this crazy thing together. .*

The relationship between the lead boater and the blind paddler or disabled paddler - in my opinion and I feel strongly about this - it should surpass kayaking. You don't need to be best friends, but you should have confidence in each other and know each other well.

Swapping personal stories, connecting early on in the trip, reaching out to them and getting a good feel for who they are so you can approach leading them in a holistic way – it's all very important. You need to understand that this guy has been through some stressful situations in his life - and he's going to handle big water better if you relate to him in a way specific to how he looks at the world around him.

If you can do that, that person is going to be a lot more likely to enjoy it and have a good time. To me, that's the most important thing, to be able to look back on a trip and remember having fun. Yes, it's great that the trip was safe and there were no injuries - that's awesome, but what you're going to remember is the fun you have, the laughs and smiles and the feeling of accomplishing something really cool That's a two way street - the blind paddler shouldn't be the only one having fun. You should be having fun, and you should be sharing that fun together.

But we shared more than that on the trip. Lonnie did time in the military as well, and there's something ingrained in everyone that goes through that motivates them to teach the people that are coming up next – in other words, be a mentor. I would tell him things in my life that were going on and he would listen. He would never give me direct suggestions, but he would ask questions about my decisions, like "Why do you want to do that?" "Is that what will make you happy?" Those kinds of questions – insightful questions that made me rethink things.

He asked me to talk about my time in the military and the scary stuff that happened while I was overseas. It's funny because I never really talk to anybody about that. I don't think it's because I'm afraid to – it just never comes up and there's never an appropriate time. With him, I felt like it was okay. I felt like we had a strong enough bond in a strange enough situation where it was appropriate to talk about it. And he was a great listener. It was huge. To hear affirmation from someone that does understand that kind of stress, to hear Lonnie say "You're doing good, you're doing fine, that's normal," that was huge for me.

Lonnie always thanks me for taking him down the canyon...but I felt like he was the one doing me a favor the entire way.

One of the humbling things about a lot of these trips is that a lot of these guys truly have opened up to me. Alex did tell me some things. Mike did too. When I would hear what people like them experienced at such a young age – well, I would just go back to my tent and say a prayer to help them let it all go and learn to put it in the perspective.

I remember telling them, "These things are always going to be a part of you, but you can't let them define you." You don't have to forget. It's all right to have the feelings that you have. Because it's a part of your life's experience."

These are hard things to talk about. To think of these guys having the faith and confidence to share these painful memories and emotions with me – well, it's a privilege and an honor. I think a big part of it is that I just listen to what they have to say. You don't tell them they're right or wrong. How can you judge them? I can remember telling some of them, as we sat around the campfire, "You can have two people in the same place, at the same time, and they both get the same injury, go through the same events – but both people come out of it very differently, because none of us are exactly the same. You can never, ever fully walk in another man's shoes."

That's why you don't judge them for how they react in trying circumstances. Instead, you applaud them for being able to carry the burden they're carrying. I think about that with all these young men and women.

> Joe: *What's great about Lonnie is that he works to take the high road no matter what disappointments there are. We didn't get much publicity when Lonnie did the Grand Canyon trip. It was around the same time that wonderful young lady Diana Nyad did her famous swim from Cuba to Florida – that got international attention. But here's Lonnie, this blind veteran doing this amazing feat with only one year's training, 14 days experience on whitewater. I know some of the best kayakers in the world – you can go anywhere in the world and people know these guys' names. When I talk to them about what Lonnie did, it just stuns them. They're like, "you're kidding me? In a year, he learned how to roll and how to run? And did the Grand Canyon?"*
>
> *He did this amazing thing and he's not known. And still, he's trying to use this as an opportunity to help others, he's out there helping us raise money and put butts in boats. It's not easy to be on the high road. But Lonnie?*
>
> *He owns it, man.*

Marking the achievement.
(Photo by Mike Bradley)

The People Who Made It All Possible

In 2014, I did my second trip down the Colorado River. A very different experience because I had so much more confidence this time around. And a lot more rest – because I camped farther away from the river, so the sound of the rapids didn't keep me up all night (and also took some books on tape!). This time, I also had a brand new kayak and gear, so there were no unexpected equipment failures. Didn't swim at all - I didn't even hardly get my nose wet in Lava Falls, except for one time when I paddled into an eddy after making it through the falls. I even ran about 5 or 6 of the rapids without a guide at all and did a few backwards, just like Alex did on the trip with me.

I am blessed to reach this awesome point in my life. If you've read this whole book, you know there was a time, shortly after I was blinded in the accident, that I was afraid to even mow the lawn by myself. My little girl Bug inspired me to do that – just as my other two girls also helped their daddy enormously on a day-to-day basis. But they were just the first in a long string of people who would encourage, inspire and guide me towards living a rich, full life, the kind of life I initially thought could never happen.

I've worked on roofs, I've used chain saws, I've gone rock climbing, I've skied down mountains and I've kayaked the Grand Canyon. These aren't things blind people are expected to be able to do. But I believe limitations are meant to be overcome. And I do continue to hope that every wonderful thing I'm able to achieve serves as an example for those who think their life has reached a dead end that they can't get past. They just have to be willing to try – and humble enough to seek out those who can help them overcome those pesky walls standing in their way.

My dad liked to tell people, after I got shot in that accident, that the reason that blindness was my only lasting injury was because my eyes were the only thing between my ears. Well, I do have to say that I have brains enough to know that I couldn't have done what I've done without the wonderful gifts the good Lord has given me and the help of those he placed in my life.

I absolutely want to thank everyone who has come into my life and been a part of assisting and encouraging me through my endeavors. So many people have helped me along the way; so many that I couldn't possibly mention everyone. The overwhelming support from all will never be forgotten.

I especially have to thank my three beautiful daughters Courtney, Ashley, and Taylor first and foremost - they are my life. I can't begin to put into words how much they mean to me and how much I love them. I am so very proud of the young women they've become – and I could write a whole second book on how much each of them has done for me.

I also want to thank my parents and my brother Larry for their pivotal roles in my life – not to mention my uncles, aunts and 17 first cousins and 2 second cousins (13 on my dad's side, 6 on my mother's side), who are like brothers and sisters to me. All of them were there for me when I needed them. I'd like to give my cousin David Bedwell a special thank you for always being there. No matter what I need, I can always count on David. And to Darlene Pirtle who is a part of my life, many thanks for standing by me with patience and support through my adventures.

I would also like to thank the 15 people, who helped guide and support me during my first trip down the Colorado River through the Grand Canyon. They are listed in alphabetical order below:

Michael Bradley – US Army

Kelly Collins – Raft Guide

Ashley Crandall – US Army

Steven Fullers – US Army

Eric Guzman – US Marine, US Army

Marc Huster - Raft Guide

Alex Nielson – US Navy

Paul Noeth - US Army

Dale Osborn – TRR Trip Coordinator

Michael Plourde - US Army

Leonard (Chip) Sell – US Army

Max Schultz – Raft Guide

Jahzeel Sequeira – US Navy

Peter Winn - Trip Advisor

Carmen Winn - Trip Leader

From left to right: Dale Osborn, Kelly Collins, Max Schultz, Carmen Winn, Marc Huster, Ashley Crandall, Peter Winn, Steven Fullers, Jahzeel Sequeira, Mike Bradley, Lonnie Bedwell, Alex Nielson, Chip Sell, Eric Guzman, Michael Plourde, Paul Noeth
(Photo provided by Dale Osborn)

I also want to thank Richard Seppala and Joel Canfield. Without Richard, this book never would have happened and without Joel, it never would have gotten written. And finally, an extra big thank you to Joe Mornini, who made the entire trip possible in the first place.

I thank them one and all – and I thank you for taking the time to read my story.

Finally, I urge you to support the great group at Team River Runner (visit them at www.teamriverrunner.org), so they can continue to help the men and women who gave up so much for us here in America.

About the Authors

Lonnie Bedwell

Lonnie Ray Bedwell was born in 1965 in Sullivan, Indiana. He grew up in nearby Pleasantville, a bustling metropolis with a population of approximately 120 people. Lonnie graduated from Union High School in 1983, then attended Vincennes University in Vincennes, Indiana, where he received a degree in Robotics.

After graduating from college, Lonnie enlisted in the U.S. Navy, where he served as a crew member on the USS Oklahoma City SSM723 submarine. After a nine year hitch, Lonnie moved back to Indiana where he worked as a supervisor at the Destec power plant and also served with the National Guard.

In May of 1997, Lonnie lost his sight in an almost-fatal hunting accident. Determined not to let his disability define him, Lonnie took on construction work as a hobby and built or assisted in the building of numerous homes as well as many renovations, despite the reluctance of some to put a blind man on a roof. During this period of time, Lonnie was also a single father to his three daughters, Courtney, Ashley and Taylor, whom he taught to cook, shoot and drive.

In late 2009, after his youngest daughter graduated high school, Lonnie sought more resources to help him live independently at the Veterans Administration's Central Blind Rehabilitation Center, located at Edward Hines, Jr. VA Hospital in Chicago, Illinois. There, he began participating in VA adaptive sports programs designed primarily for wounded and injured soldiers returning from Iraq and Afghanistan. As Lonnie was not wounded in combat, at first he was barred from such activities; however, organizations such as the Wounded Warrior Project saw the value of his working in a mentorship role for other vets.

For the first time in his life, Lonnie engaged in activities such as rock climbing, cycling and snow skiing - where he hurtled down black diamond ski slopes behind a guide loudly ringing a cow bell for him to follow (a sport he continues to pursue - recently, he was clocked at 60 mph going down a ski slope in Aspen).

In March of 2012, Lonnie had his first experience kayaking. Joe Mornini, co-founder of Team River Runner, a nonprofit dedicated to giving disabled veterans access to paddling sports, recognized Lonnie's skills and leadership qualities and trained him to take on the challenge of becoming the first blind person ever to kayak the whitewater rapids on the Colorado River through the Grand Canyon. In August of 2013, Lonnie successfully completed the 226 mile journey, with the help of his lead guide Alex Nielson, as well as his other two guides, Mike Bradley and Leonard "Chip" Sell.

Lonnie truly believes this achievement is meaningless unless he continues to "pay it forward" - by helping other disabled veterans enjoy full and meaningful lives. He still resides in Indiana and is definitely on the lookout for his next big challenge.

Find out more about Lonnie at www.LonnieBedwell.com.

Joel Canfield

Joel is a New York-based ghostwriter and screenwriter who, along with his wife, Lisa Canfield, co-authored *What's Driving You???: How I Overcame Abuse and Learned to Lead in the NBA*, the autobiography of pro basketball veteran Keyon Dooling, as well as many other best-sellers for other athletes, business CEOs, entrepreneurs, and even a few gangsters. Find out more about Joel at www.GetHipCreative.com.

Made in the USA
San Bernardino, CA
17 August 2015